Latin America

Development and conflict since 1945

Second edition

John Ward

Routledge
Taylor & Francis Group

LONDON AND NEW YORK

First published 1997
by Routledge
2 Park Square, Milton Park, Abingdon, Oxfordshire, OX14 4RN

Simultaneously published in the USA and Canada
by Routledge
29 West 35th Street, New York, NY 10001

Second edition first published 2004

Routledge is an imprint of the Taylor & Francis Group

© 1997, 2004 John Ward

Typeset in Times by
Florence Production Ltd, Stoodleigh, Devon
Printed and bound in Great Britain by
TJ International Ltd, Padstow, Cornwall

British Library Cataloguing in Publication Data
A catalogue record for this book is available from the
British Library

Library of Congress Cataloging in Publication Data
Ward, John, 1946–
 Latin America: development and conflict since 1945/
John Ward. – 2nd ed.
 p. cm. – (Making of the contemporary world)
Includes bibliographical references and index.
1. Latin America – Economic conditions – 1945– 2. Latin
America – Social conditions – 1945–1982. 3. Latin America –
Social conditions – 1982– I. Title. II. Series.
HC125.W37 2004
330.98′0033 – dc22   2003027168

ISBN 0–415–31822–X (hbk)
ISBN 0–415–31823–8 (pbk)

Contents

Illustrations

viii   *Illustrations*

Preface to the second edition

This is an enlarged and updated reissue, prepared in mid-2003, of a book written in mid-1996. The new material reflects events as they have unfolded over the intervening period, further research, and comments, gratefully received, both on the first edition and on the revised text.

Acknowledgements

I am grateful to the series editors, their advisers, and the staff at Routledge, for commenting on drafts of this book. I should also like to thank my wife for her support during the process of composition.

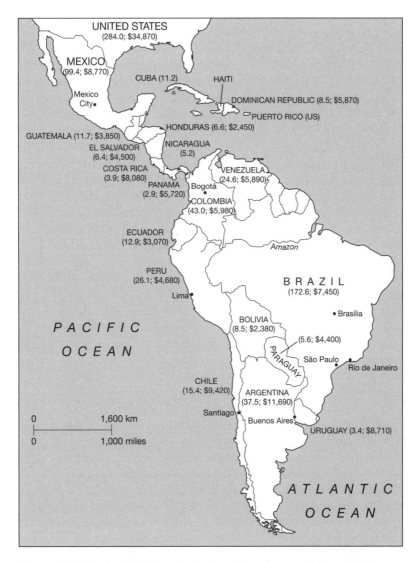

Map Latin America, 2001 (population in millions; output per head, US$, purchasing power parities)

Source: World Bank 2003: 234–5.

1 Introduction

Latin American history began in 1492 when Christopher Columbus, sponsored by the Spanish crown, led a naval expedition across the Atlantic and made landfall on various Caribbean islands. Further voyages of exploration and settlement followed. At first the newcomers concentrated their activities in the West Indies, working alluvial gold deposits and exterminating most of the indigenous inhabitants, used as forced labour. However, Spanish adventurers soon reached the mainland, where they found and quickly subjugated large 'Indian'[1] populations, concentrated in Central America and the Andean highlands of South America. These regions would become the main centres of Spain's transatlantic empire which, by 1600, stretched 6,000 miles, from what is now the southwestern US to central Chile and Argentina. For comparison, by 1750, after a century and a half of colonization, British settlers in North America had penetrated only about 200 miles inland from the eastern seaboard, along a 1,000 mile front. The Spanish conquistadors advanced so rapidly because of their eagerness to acquire the gold and silver which was available in great quantities, an aggressive military spirit, a wish to spread the Catholic Christian faith, and the weakness of the established indigenous empires (the Aztecs in Mexico, the Incas in Peru). The Spanish American economy came to be based on the extraction of tribute from the Indians, and the mining of precious metals. The colonial elite also established large agricultural estates (*haciendas*) to supply the mines, and the towns where most Spanish settlers, immigrant and locally born (creole), took up residence.

At first, the Spanish comprised a small minority among the conquered Indians. However, the diseases introduced to the Americas by the Europeans devastated Indian populations, while there was a rapid growth in the number of whites and *mestizos* (people of mixed white/Indian descent). Also, black slaves were imported from Africa.

By the early nineteenth century the population of Spanish America, totalling about 16 million, was made up roughly as follows: 18 per cent white, 28 per cent *mestizo* or *mulato* (of mixed white/black race), 42 per cent Indian, and 12 per cent black (Skidmore and Smith 2001: 25).

The coastal zone of present-day Brazil was discovered by the Portuguese in 1500 and developed during the sixteenth and seventeenth centuries as Europe's main source of sugar. From the 1690s important gold deposits began to be discovered and worked in the interior. Because Brazil's Indians were less numerous than Spanish America's, the Portuguese relied more heavily on the labour of African slaves. By the 1820s about 23 per cent of Brazil's four million population was white, 18 per cent mixed race, 50 per cent black, and 9 per cent Indian (Skidmore and Smith 2001: 25).

The racial composition of Latin American colonial society differed markedly from the patterns found in other European overseas territories. In the thirteen British North American colonies that eventually became the US, whites were an overwhelming majority and the Indians a marginal element by the eighteenth century. Black slaves accounted for about 10 per cent of the population. Alternatively, in colonial Asia and Africa whites usually remained a very small minority, unable to retain power when indigenous anti-European nationalism gathered strength after 1900. In Latin America whites and *mestizos* led the movements against Spanish and Portuguese colonial rule that brought to independence all the region, except Spain's Caribbean islands, between 1808 and the mid-1820s.[2] Latin American societies have remained more or less racially diverse and stratified to this day.

Despite their apparent natural advantages – rich mineral deposits and extensive areas of fertile land – the Latin American colonies did not achieve sustained growth in output per head of population, or in manufacturing and commercial activity as a share of output. By the early nineteenth century the region's economic development compared unfavourably with that of Britain or the US, where rapid industrialization was in progress.

Spanish America's extensive territories had proved difficult to administer effectively, and vulnerable to attack from predatory European rivals: the Dutch, the French, and the British. In both Spanish America and Brazil heavy taxation limited savings and investment. Legal restrictions and poor transport facilities limited trade. The Inquisition conducted by the Catholic Church against heresy discouraged scientific thought. Most large estates were farmed carelessly. Salaried managers, deputizing for absentee owners, supervised poorly motivated coerced labourers, usually conscripted or indebted Indians in the Spanish colonies and black slaves in Brazil. Poverty prevented the Indian communities which still controlled about half of Spanish America's agricultural land from improving their methods (Williamson 1992: 119–32, 183–90).

Latin American economic retardation was perpetuated for several decades after independence by chronic political instability. The creole elites who had shaken off European rule were split between 'Conservatives' who wanted to maintain established institutions, and 'Liberals' who sought modernizing reform, for example by cutting back the privileges of the Catholic Church. Frontier disputes broke out between several of the successor states. Mexico lost a third of its national territory (present day California, Arizona, New Mexico, and Texas) to the expansionist US. The wars of independence had severely damaged the silver mines, a main source of tax revenue during the colonial period, so governments now lacked sufficient income. Effective authority often passed to individual strongmen (*caudillos*) whose power derived from the ownership of large, landed estates and from the personal command over fighting men (Halperin Donghi 1993: 42–114; Bulmer-Thomas 1994: 19–45).

Disorder persisted until the second half of the nineteenth century. Hitherto the region's exports had been limited to silver, gold, and the few other items, such as sugar from coastal Brazil and the Caribbean, which could bear the cost of shipment to distant markets. Then, from about 1850, the demand generated by Western European and US industrialization, combined with the cheaper transport offered by railways and steam shipping, made it feasible for Latin America to send out a greater range and volume of bulk cargoes, including coffee, wool, grain, meat, cotton, nitrates, and base metals. However, landowners could only profit from these new opportunities by accepting strong central government, to secure property, mobilize labour, and attract outside money for building railways and other essential infrastructure. Some *caudillos* tried to hold out against this new model of political economy, but once in motion it usually had an irresistible momentum. The growth of foreign trade enlarged governments' tax revenues, and loans from European and US financiers, reassured by the better business prospects. Adequately paid and equipped national armies, now often with railways at their disposal, could crush regional opposition, further improving investment conditions, state finances, and domestic security.

By 1900 most Latin American countries were controlled by restricted groups of large landowners, dedicated to export expansion through collaboration with foreign capitalists, and subscribing, formally at least, to the principles of laissez-faire economic liberalism, imported from Europe. According to this doctrine, international free trade maximized prosperity, by allowing each country to specialize in products for which its resources were best suited, according to the principles of comparative advantage. So, Latin America should export raw materials in return for European and US manufactured goods. State intervention in the national economy should be kept to a minimum. The main function of government was to uphold law and order, allowing private enterprise to flourish. In practice, however, the dominant elites often secured government help when it was likely to be profitable for them, including highly illiberal repressive measures against social inferiors. Characteristic ruling oligarchies included the coffee planters of Brazil's São Paulo region, the leading influence in the country's First Republic (1889–1930), and Argentina's *estancieros,* their fortunes based on the production of wool, grain, and beef. Some governments were dominated more completely by a single man. In Mexico, where the post-independence political instability had been particularly severe, Porfirio Díaz held office as president almost continuously from 1876 until 1911.

The export booms enriched Latin America's elites, but brought little benefit to the population at large. Over the nineteenth century as a whole, average output per head did not rise significantly; in terms of economic development the region fell further behind Western Europe and North America. Liberal ideology was used as a pretext for taking collectively held land from Indian communities and adding it to the *haciendas.* The strengthened armies and police forces were put at the service of employers in recruiting and disciplining workers. Cash crops for sale overseas encroached on the growing of food for local consumption. Competition from cheaper factory-made goods, imported or national, destroyed handicrafts and the employment which they provided. The widening income disparities between rich and poor held back industrialization by limiting the demand for simple manufactures. The elites preferred luxury imports (Bulmer-Thomas 1994: 83–154, 410–14).

Nevertheless, some industrial and commercial growth did occur in Latin America, fostering urban 'middle sectors' that eventually became strong enough to challenge the export oligarchies. With growing affluence the elites required more doctors, lawyers, shopkeepers, and other functionaries. Estate owners were reluctant to tax their own income or property, so they unintentionally fostered industrialization by using duties on imported goods as a main source of government revenue. Exports often required some processing before being shipped abroad. Transport equipment had to be maintained. For example, the establishment of meat packing plants (*frigoríficos*) and railway repair workshops contributed to the growth of Buenos Aires, Argentina's capital.

As urban populations became more numerous, they grew increasingly self-confident, assertive, and critical of elite rule, with its alleged subordination of national interests to foreigners. The Mexican Revolution (1910–20) provided a reforming, nationalist example for Latin America as a whole. The First World War limited the supply of imported manufactured goods and gave some extra encouragement to industrialization within the region. The next major impetus to social and political change was provided by the international economic depression that followed the 1929 New York stock exchange crash. Although Latin America's foreign trade fell sharply, in most of the region's larger countries economic activity soon recovered. The decline of raw material exports made imported manufactures scarcer and more expensive, so national industry grew faster than before, by enlarging its share of the home market. Then, the Second World War revived export earnings. Latin America lay at a distance from the main theatres of armed conflict, comparatively well placed to help meet the demands of the US and its allies for metals, oil, and other strategic materials (Bulmer-Thomas 1994: 155–257).

Latin American manufacturing growth accelerated after 1945, with increasingly active government support through deliberate policies of import substituting industrialization (ISI). Higher protective duties and new controls were imposed to exclude foreign manufactures. Public enterprises were made responsible for some of the more ambitious industrial projects. At first, state-supported ISI yielded impressive results, but by the later 1950s the strategy had begun to show various limitations. The new or enlarged industries were quite successful in meeting national demand for the simpler consumer products, but required considerable imports of machinery and raw materials. As world commodity prices began to fall after the end of the Korean War in 1953, Latin American earnings from raw material exports failed to keep pace with import needs, and many countries incurred persistent balance of payments deficits. Higher inflation impaired the competitiveness of Latin American exports, aggravating balance of payments problems. Social conflict intensified as workers struggled to secure pay increases that would offset anticipated declines in the value of money. By the early 1960s ISI was in crisis.

Latin American countries responded with a range of adjustments or reforms, their detail and emphasis differing according to local circumstances (Chapters 2 and 5). Nevertheless, although economic growth continued during the 1960s and 1970s, balance of payments deficits widened further, so by 1980 Latin America had become heavily reliant on loans from foreign banks. Then the region suffered a severe recession, precipitated by a downturn in the world economy, depressed prices for raw material exports, and higher international interest rates. The debt crisis caused widespread disillusionment with ISI as a development strategy, pursued in its various modified forms, since the 1960s. Also, foreign creditors were able to impose their view that efficiency would be improved by reducing government intervention and opening up national economies to competitive forces. Thus, a fashion for economic liberalization took hold in Latin America during the later 1980s, cutting back the protective tariffs, the state agencies, and the state controls built up since 1945. Yet, so far the results from liberalization have been disappointing. In most Latin American countries output per head fell during the 1980s, the region's 'lost decade'. The early 1990s brought a modest recovery, but this was soon threatened by renewed financial difficulties, and the current outlook is most uncertain (Bulmer-Thomas 1994: 155–409; ECLAC 2000, 2002).

Latin American attempts to promote economic development since 1945 have been accompanied by persistent political instability. Although there are considerable differences between countries, the common sequence runs as follows. As a result of the post-1929 crisis in world trade and finance, many ruling export oligarchies lost power, often through a military coup. With the growth of manufacturing and of cities, governments increasingly took on a populist character. They represented, or claimed to represent, a broad coalition of mainly urban supporters: the professional and service middle classes, industrialists, and manual workers. Populist leaders based their appeal on nationalist measures against foreign business interests, and rhetorical attacks against landowning elites, condemned as 'backward', 'feudal', and the foreigners' allies. However, few substantive measures were taken to break up the big, landed estates, and conservative landowners remained a significant political force, especially when they could enlist support from the middle classes and the military, alarmed at populist excesses. Mexico (1910–20) and Bolivia

(1952) were exceptional in undergoing broadly based revolutionary upheavals that yielded major agrarian reforms, though even here considerable inequalities in landownership remained. Then, in 1959, forces led by Fidel Castro overthrew the Cuban dictator Batista. Castro's regime soon became socialist, closely allying Cuba with the Soviet Union against the US, and broadcasting revolutionary propaganda to the rest of Latin America.

The threat from Cuba and the crisis of ISI provoked military coups against elected civilian governments in Brazil (1964) and Argentina (1962, 1966). The 'bureaucratic-authoritarian' military regimes established here claimed to be above politics, and capable of putting ISI on a more disciplined, sustainable basis, by imposing austerity programmes. Elsewhere, for example in Peru (1968) and Ecuador (1972), the military took charge, committed to a more 'left-populist' line. In Chile, disappointment with civilian politicians' attempts at moderate reform during the 1960s led, in 1970, to the election as president of Salvador Allende, a professed Marxist. After three turbulent years, power was seized by an especially harsh military dictatorship, led by General Pinochet. Mexico gave an impression of stability under its governing party (the PRI), established by the 1910–20 revolution. However, economic difficulties and social discontent weakened the PRI's authority, so policy implementation became increasingly erratic.

In most of the small Central American republics restricted landholding elites were still dominant, often ruling through the armed forces. A single family, the Somozas, controlled Nicaragua. During the 1960s and 1970s these oligarchies had to contend with growing popular unrest, mainly in the form of rural and peasant-based uprisings. The Sandinista guerrillas overthrew Nicaragua's Somoza regime in 1979. Rural insurrectionary movements also affected parts of Colombia, Peru, and Mexico. In the Southern Cone (Argentina, Uruguay, Chile) ultra-left 'urban guerrillas' were more conspicuous. The kidnappings, bombings, and armed attacks perpetrated by these small groups of young, predominantly middle-class, activists served as another pretext for military intervention, to root out terrorism (Halperin Donghi 1993: 292–400; Skidmore and Smith 2001).

From the early 1980s violent social conflict moderated over most of the region, and politics became less sharply polarized. The debt crisis brought a return to democracy as discredited military regimes gave up office. Their civilian successors were, on the whole, cautious and restrained, by the standards of pre-1960 populism. In a number of cases presidents secured re-election, despite implementing painful measures for economic stabilization. Urban guerrilla activity, effectively crushed by 1980, showed no signs of revival. So, at least up to the mid-1990s it seemed that painful experience might have established a more secure consensus, bringing to an end the abrupt swings between populist, authoritarian, and radical alternatives that characterized the 1945–80 period. Subsequently, however, some republics experienced political instability once again, through public dissatisfaction with the results of free market reform.

Table 1.1 gives some recent indicators of Latin America's economic standing. Output per head of population is estimated on a purchasing power parity basis, which takes account of international differences in price levels. (For comparative purposes this method is preferable to calculations of the type often used, based on national currencies at official or market exchange rates.)

The averages for Latin America cover wide variations between the richer and poorer countries, for example between Chile (2001 output per head $9,420) or Mexico ($8,770) and Honduras ($2,450) or Bolivia ($2,380). Latin America's output per head is much lower than that of the developed 'First World'. Yet, despite the post-1980 problems, at the turn of the century the region was still quite prosperous

Table 1.1 Comparative indicators of development and welfare, *c.*2001

	Output per head (in US$)	Mortality rate[a] of children under 5 years old
Developing countries	3,930	85
Latin America	7,070	37
East Asia	4,040	45
South Asia[b]	2,300	96
Sub-Saharan Africa	1,620	162
Middle East[c]	5,230	54
Developed countries		
United Kingdom	24,460	7
US	34,870	9

Source: World Bank 2003: 234–5.

Notes:
a Rate per 1,000.
b India, Pakistan, Bangladesh, Nepal, Sri Lanka, Afghanistan, Maldives. India is by far the largest country in this group and dominates the regional average.
c Including North Africa.

Table 1.2 Annual rates of growth in output per head of population: main world regions, 1950–2002 (%)

	1950–9	1960–9	1970–9	1980–9	1990–9	2000–2
Developing countries	2.8	2.7	2.9	1.9	3.1	3.0
Latin America	2.2	2.4	3.0	−0.7	1.7	−0.3
East Asia	3.8	2.2	4.0	4.9	5.1	5.0
NICs	4.0	6.4	7.6	6.3	5.0	3.4
China	4.4	1.5	3.1	5.7	6.5	6.8
ASEAN 3[a]	2.0	2.5	4.6	3.9	2.9	2.3
South Asia	1.7	1.7	0.8	3.2	3.7	3.1
India	2.0	1.4	0.8	3.4	3.8	3.1
Sub-Saharan Africa	1.9	2.9	0.3	−1.3	−0.2	0.6
Middle East	3.0	4.4	3.0	−0.7	0.8	2.1
Developed countries	3.3	4.1	2.5	2.3	1.8	1.4

Sources: Maddison 2001; IMF 2003.

Note: a Thailand, Malaysia, Indonesia

by the standards of 'Third World' developing countries. Latin America's output per head grew roughly three-fold between 1913 and 1980 (Bulmer-Thomas 1994: 444), an increase similar to the First World's over the same period.

However, other criteria put Latin America in a more unfavourable light. While the region's average output per head in 2001 was still the highest in the Third World, since the 1960s East Asia's has been growing at a much faster rate (Table 1.2). Also, the average for East Asia is dominated by China, a large and still relatively poor country (2001 output per head $4,260). Much higher levels of prosperity have been achieved by certain smaller East Asian territories, sometimes referred to as the 'Gang of Four' or 'Baby Tigers': South Korea ($18,110), Taiwan ($23,000), Singapore ($24,910), and Hong Kong ($26,050). The success of these 'newly industrialized countries' (NICs) was associated with the production of manufactured goods for export, and entailed annual growth in output per head at rates of 6–8 per cent. Since the 1970s their pattern of rapid export-led development has been imitated by China, Vietnam, and, with rather more modest long-term success, some capitalist South-east Asian countries (Thailand, Malaysia, Indonesia), termed here the ASEAN 3, after a regional trade group. Over recent years India's economic performance has also significantly improved through the relaxation of ISI. Finally, Latin America has made less progress than East Asia in raising standards of welfare, such as nutrition and child mortality.

Therefore, Latin American history is commonly seen as one of 'unfulfilled promise' (Bulmer-Thomas 1994: 410). The region has failed to achieve First World living standards, despite an abundance of natural resources, and failed to establish a tradition of stable democratic government, despite the ideals proclaimed by the early nineteenth-century independence movements.

Theoretical perspectives

The chapter so far has concentrated on matters of fact. We shall now raise issues of interpretation, by sketching out various theories or explanations that may be relevant to understanding Latin America's current difficulties and its historical past.

During the oligarchical period, Latin American elites hoped to improve their countries' relative economic status by promoting exports. However, it was widely believed that severe, perhaps insuperable obstacles to achieving US or Western European levels of development were posed by the effects of the tropical climate in discouraging hard work, and by the natural inferiority of the region's large non-white populations. Such climatic or racial determinism is no longer accepted.

Structuralism

A more sophisticated view was offered by structuralism, a body of thinking developed in the 1940s and 1950s to justify ISI. The approach came to be particularly associated with the Argentine economist Raúl Prebisch and one of the main vehicles for his influence, the Economic Commission for Latin America (ECLA), a United Nations agency established in 1948. (The term structuralism derived from a subsidiary argument, which attributed the high inflation often generated by ISI to aspects of Latin American economic *structure*.) Prebisch argued that for various reasons Latin America was suffering from a long-term decline in the price of its raw material exports relative to the price of the manufactured goods imported from the advanced industrial economies. The share of food and other basic commodities in developed countries' consumer spending was declining as incomes rose. Synthetic substitutes were being developed for many raw materials. The limited number of industrial firms made possible monopolistic or semi-monopolistic restraints on price competition, and industrial workers were organized in powerful trade unions. Therefore, while in manufacturing technical progress benefited producers, through higher profits and wages, in primary commodity sectors it benefited consumers, through lower prices. This invalidated the claim of liberal economists that all countries gained equally from free world trade and the international division of labour, according to the principle of comparative advantage. Latin America had been affected by a pattern of 'unequal exchange'. The region could only escape from its subordinate, 'peripheral' status and catch up with the developed 'centre', by strengthening its own industry, using whatever degree of government support might be required (Bethell 1994a: 393–432).

Modernization theory

Structuralist analysis and ISI policy received support during the 1950s from the 'modernization theory' expounded by many US-based social scientists, who assumed that Latin American countries (and the Third World as a whole) were beginning a process of change already completed by the advanced industrial countries. The introduction of superior First World technologies would raise production per head. Industry's share of national output would rise, and agriculture's would decline. The growth of towns would allow people to escape from the ignorance and apathy allegedly characteristic of 'traditional' rural life, dominated in Latin America by archaic 'feudal' estates, to become more educated, ambitious, innovative, and enterprising. 'Modernized' social attitudes, rising prosperity, and a growing middle class, would provide a secure basis for democracy, as an alternative to 'traditional' dictatorships and oligarchies (Cubitt 1995: 32–5).

However, in the 1960s both structuralism and modernization theory came to be seen as over-optimistic. Apart from ISI's obvious economic weaknesses, its social and political consequences also caused alarm. The opportunities offered by industrialization attracted waves of migrants into the towns from the countryside, though the new factories provided employment for only a small minority. Millions had to eke out a living from casual 'informal sector' occupations, for example street trading or building work, and find housing in the shanty towns that proliferated around the major cities. Urbanization of this type did not offer a likely basis for the smooth, conflict-free progress envisaged by modernization theory. The advent of bureaucratic-authoritarian military regimes contradicted arguments that economic development would strengthen democracy.

Dependency theory

These trends stimulated the formulation of dependency theory, quasi-Marxist and strongly anti-capitalist in its assumptions. Dependency theory also drew encouragement from a general radical mood, inspired by the Cuban revolution, by the campaign for black civil rights in the US, and by opposition to US military involvement in Vietnam. *Dependentistas* accepted the ECLA thesis that ISI was necessary to end the 'unequal exchange' which Latin America had suffered in its foreign trade. However, they rejected structuralist attempts to base development on partnership between government and a private capitalist sector. In practice Latin American industrialization had come to rely heavily on manufacturing investment by large US and European firms, the so-called multinational or transnational corporations (MNCs, TNCs). According to dependency theory the MNCs used monopoly power to extract large profits and royalty payments from the countries in which they operated. The firms equipped their Latin American branch factories with costly imported machinery, developed for use in developed economies where high wage levels required labour-saving technology. Thus, further pressure was put on Latin America's balance of payments. The investment created few jobs, but superseded existing labour-intensive operations, so instead of the widely spread prosperity anticipated by modernization theory, unemployment and inequality were made worse. MNC penetration displaced or incorporated nationally owned firms, preventing profit accumulation for reinvestment in Latin America and the growth there of a middle class. The swing towards authoritarian military rule in the 1960s was interpreted as resulting from the concern of narrow indigenous 'collaborating elites' to reassure their foreign allies by repressing national labour movements. Dependency theory was first evolved for Latin America, and then applied to Third World countries in general. It claimed that they could only achieve true development through socialist revolution and exit from the international capitalist economy, following the Cuban and Chinese examples (Bethell 1994a: 432–54; Cubitt 1995: 35–41).

After enjoying a phase of influence during the later 1960s and early 1970s, dependency theory fell into disrepute. The enthusiasm for radical causes, characteristic of the period, waned. Attempts at giving ideas of socialist self-sufficiency practical effect had disappointing results on Cuba, for example, and disastrous effects elsewhere, most notoriously in Cambodia and Ethiopia. Above all, the increasingly conspicuous success of the East Asian NICs, based on vigorous participation in the international economy, challenged the assumption that First World capitalism is a malign, exploitative force, from which the Third World should distance itself.

Neoliberalism

The decline of dependency theory has been balanced by the resurgence of free-market ideology, now usually termed neoliberalism. In the developed countries liberal laissez-faire was discredited by the depression of the 1930s and by the effectiveness of government action in mobilizing resources during the Second World War. Thus, after 1945 opinion favoured a 'mixed' economy, combining capitalism with substantial state participation and management. The consensus lasted until about 1970, when the US and Western Europe began to experience declining rates of output growth, accompanied by rising inflation and unemployment. The malaise could be plausibly attributed to excessive government 'interference', so economic liberalism came back into favour, after surviving for the duration as a minority faith in academic circles. The neoliberal programme, known from its political leaders as 'Thatcherism' in Britain, and 'Reaganomics' in the US, aimed at reinvigorating capitalist enterprise, by tax cuts, deregulation, and the transfer of state undertakings to private ownership (privatization).

These successive currents of First World opinion reached Latin America, and the Third World at large. The fashion for state intervention established in the 1940s encouraged ECLA structuralist ideas and ISI policies; its erosion three decades later encouraged the turn towards economic liberalization. Neoliberalism has gained ground in Latin America partly through local disillusionment with ISI, brought to a head by the debt crisis. Also, many Latin American economists are trained at US or Western European universities. Finally, since 1982 Latin America's financial plight has given leverage to the US government, working together with the IMF (International Monetary Fund) and the World Bank, agencies headquartered in Washington, DC. This coalition urging neoliberal reforms on developing countries, as a prerequisite for further loans, is sometimes termed the Washington consensus (Williamson 1990).

Neoliberals admire the East Asian model of rapid outward-looking development, and recommend it as an example for Latin America to follow. They cite the policy reforms initiated about 1960 by Taiwan and South Korea which repudiated ISI and launched manufacturing export drives. According to the neoliberal analysis, at least in its early and more dogmatic versions, these countries' subsequent economic success was achieved by minimizing detailed government intervention with the 'distortions' which it causes, and allowing market forces free play (Balassa *et al.* 1986). Thus, it is alleged, the basis was laid for vigorous export-led growth. In contrast, Latin America suffered because policy there remained too inward-looking and interventionist. Neoliberals also emphasize the benefits that the East Asian NICs enjoyed from fiscal prudence. Balanced government budgets, or at least small deficits, helped ensure low inflation and a stable macroeconomic environment for private sector business.

East Asia's economic dynamism has helped to discredit dependency theory, but there are many who dislike the neoliberal alternative, and challenge its gloss on the region's history. Critics of neoliberalism will be referred to collectively as statists, though the term covers different shades of opinion (see below). Statists have gathered evidence that governments took a highly active role in East Asian industrialization, a point that most neoliberals now concede, especially for South Korea (World Bank 1987: 71). Therefore, the real contrast may not be between East Asia's free market success and futile Latin American *dirigisme*, but between effective East Asian and ineffective Latin American state intervention. If so, then further problems arise. What specific measures have proved most useful? And why should governments have been better able to sustain them in East Asia than in Latin America? Debate over these matters, conducted through comparison of the two regions, informed much work on recent Latin American history published during the 1980s and early 1990s (Morawetz 1981; Lin 1989; Gereffi and Wyman 1990; Haggard 1990; Banuri 1991; Hewitt *et al.* 1992), and the comparative theme recurs at a number of points in this book. Of the four original 'Baby Tigers', the city states Hong Kong and Singapore are quite distinctive in structure, so South Korea and, more occasionally, Taiwan will serve as the main NIC reference points. The East Asian NICs and most Latin American countries shared the same general objectives, of achieving economic development and rising income per head through industrialization. Nevertheless, the NICs' strategies differed from Latin America's in their detail, and proved much more successful. A substantial comparative literature drawing in the larger Asian countries, 'second tier' followers of the NIC path, has yet to develop. However, their experience cannot be left out, and is mentioned occasionally here.

Neo-structuralism

Since the late 1980s, debate over Latin America's economic problems has become a little less polarized, because some points of the neoliberal diagnosis have won fuller acceptance in the region through a hybrid approach covered by the rather clumsy terms neo-structuralism or *cepalismo*. This perspective found particular favour among technocrats associated with the ECLA (CEPAL), once the main centre of structuralist thought, and influenced some reforming centre-left governments, such as the Concertación alliance that took power after the end of military rule in Chile (1990), and the Cardoso presidencies in Brazil (1995–2002). Neo-structuralism accepts the need to engage more actively in world trade, to attract foreign investment, and to leave most productive activity to private sector business. Macroeconomic stability is an important objective. Opinion shifted on these points in Latin America partly because attempts at persevering with ISI after the 1982 debt crisis had poor results (see below).

However, neo-structuralism still differs from neoliberalism in arguing for strong state action to support private sector enterprise, especially with technological improvement, and to mitigate Latin America's extreme income inequality through bold redistributive measures. Higher taxes on the rich should fund improved welfare services for the poor. Neo-structuralists put great faith in the benefits likely to come from reformed, enlightened government. Neo-liberals eventually saw the need for greater state supervision to check capitalist excesses and abuses, but still doubt whether the public sector can usefully take a more direct interventionist role as an agent of technical progress. Neoliberals also recognize the economic value of welfare services that ensure a healthy, well-educated labour force, and of 'safety net' poverty relief to ease post-ISI adjustment, but claim that the careful targeting of benefits can hold down costs. Ambitious redistribution programmes should be avoided. Such measures are likely to entail political conflict, government budget deficits, and extra burdens on productive enterprise. The best hope for reduced income inequality and improved welfare over the long term, neoliberals believe, is through 'trickle down' and rapid export-led growth along East Asian lines. The extra demand for labour will, sooner or later, push up wages (Green 1995: 188–91, 244–9).

The grassroots left and 'post-modernism'

Neo-structuralism is a doctrine of the political middle ground, favoured by highly educated elites that have good chances of gaining state power. But other more radical views remain current, even though revolutionary Marxism and dependency theory have lost their previous vigour. At the academic level, neoliberalism and neo-structuralism focus on economics. Discussion of the issues raised has involved economists and economic historians. Other disciplines (political science, sociology, social anthropology) that were, for a time, more receptive to dependency theory, have coped with its decline by developing an alternative approach that is sometimes described as 'post-modernist' (Cubitt 1995: 47–9), though 'post-Marxist' or 'neo-populist' might be more appropriate. The term post-modernism derives from some once fashionable ideas in philosophy, linguistics, and literary analysis, used to argue that no all-embracing theory can accommodate the cultural diversity of human behaviour. This view contrasts with Marxist interpretations, which categorized society in terms of a few classes, based on economic interest, and made conflict between them determine historical change. Though 'left' in spirit, and strongly hostile to neoliberalism, the post-modernist perspective is loosely defined and eclectic. It takes a sympathetic interest in a wide variety of subordinate popular elements, often localized and small-scale, which challenge 'establishment' capitalist orthodoxy. They include neighbourhood self-help groups among the poor, and activists on environmental issues. There is also a related concern with gender and with women's role in society, preoccupations of the feminist movement that grew from the 1960s' radical upsurge. Writers influenced by post-modernist thinking believe that the recent proliferation in Latin America of local-level movements, often involving women, indigenous peoples, and other hitherto marginalized categories, represents a hopeful trend. Perhaps grassroots, 'bottom up' approaches to development needs can succeed where clumsy, technocratic, 'top down' projects failed (Green 1991; Green 1995: 192–6). Since the mid-1990s such views have been expressed through 'anti-globalization' protest, both in Latin America and further afield.

Here, we use the term statist to cover all critics of neoliberalism, distinguishing neo-structuralist and radical, leftist, or post-modernist arguments where necessary.

Plan of this book

The following discussion has these issues in mind. The primary subject is recent economic history, but we must locate the economics within a larger set of interrelated themes, and recognize how modern phenomena often have more remote historical origins. Chapters 2 and 3 pursue the topic of economic development, defined narrowly as the growth in output per head of population. (The welfare aspects of development are considered separately, in Chapter 6.) ISI as practised in Latin America after 1945 proved a deeply flawed strategy, inferior to the more outward-looking, export-oriented approach adopted by the East Asian NICs. As a result, Latin America became over-reliant on foreign capital, and was severely affected by the debt crisis of the early 1980s. However, the remedies applied in the region have had major limitations as a basis for securing recovery and, partly for this reason, the post-1980 economic slow-down has been prolonged.

Chapter 4 examines the position of Latin America in the wider world. While dependency theory as an elaborated doctrine has lost influence, it still keeps some adherents. For example, according to one widely used text, the damage caused by the application of neo-liberal policy to Latin America's problems 'suggests that in all essential respects the economic and social crisis of the area has worsened and its dependency vis-à-vis the core capitalist powers has deepened' (Keen and Haynes 2000: x). More generally, many authors still consider that the region has suffered particular dis-advantages in its international relations, perhaps through the close proximity of the US as an overbearing superpower. However, it is argued here that external pressures should not be seen as a main cause of the region's difficulties since 1945.

Chapter 5, therefore, reviews the course of social change and political conflict within Latin America over the last half century. Political instability has resulted, above all, from the failure of govern-ments to satisfy aspirations for sustained economic growth, in a region marked by exceptionally wide disparities between rich and poor. Such inequality derived originally from the racial stratification and concentrated landownership established by a distinctive pattern of European rule, but has been aggravated by ISI. Unstable, erratic government has, in turn, further impaired economic performance. Latin America differs markedly on this point from East Asia, where, for historical reasons, societies are more cohesive, homogeneous, and egalitarian, and where strong, purposeful governments have been better able to implement coherent development strategies (Gereffi and Wyman 1990: 139–204).

Latin American inequality has had other economic consequences, through its effects on social welfare (Chapter 6). With a large share of income going to wealthy elites, much of the population has been left without adequate health care and education, to the detriment of labour efficiency. A criticism levelled against liberalization is that it aggravates the problem of labour force 'quality', by requiring cuts in government spending and other adjustments that fall most severely on the poor. Neoliberals reply that their policies will promote welfare through the employment generated by labour-intensive economic growth of the East Asian type. They also argue that the poor can be protected from spending reductions by deploying available resources more selectively. In fact, some social indicators have continued to improve since the early 1980s, even when average income per head fell. Local-level popular action may have limited the damaging welfare effects of the debt crisis, partly justifying the post-modernist left's stress of the value of grassroots mobilization. However, 'bottom up' initiatives cannot, by themselves, go very far towards solving the region's development problems.

The period since 1945 has brought some improvement in the status of Latin American women (Chapter 7). However, the social progress represented by female emancipation may also entail economic costs. Considerable use has been made of women workers in East Asian manufacturing, where they have been obliged by patriarchal, discriminatory attitudes to accept rigorous discipline, and much lower rates of pay than those received by equally skilled men. In Latin American industry, on the other hand, female participation has remained relatively low, a significant competitive disadvantage. Furthermore, over the last thirty years, feminist movements have grown up in the region, their position enhanced by the return to democratic politics. This is probably limiting the recruitment of Latin American women as cheap, flexible, docile labour for export manufacturing, along East Asian lines.

Recently, Latin American environmental issues (Chapter 8) have attracted much notice, especially through First World concern over the destruction of the Amazonian rainforest. The road building, cattle ranching, power generation, and mining projects associated with deforestation may represent examples of the misdirected investment that led to the debt crisis of the early 1980s. Accelerating environmental degradation may have played an important role in aggravating the subsequent recession; critics of neoliberalism claim that globalization is severely depleting natural resources. However, these points are open to dispute.

The book concludes with some remarks on Latin America's current situation, in the light of the historical record (Chapter 9). Neoliberals claim that the economic upturn achieved by the region since the early 1990s shows that their recommendations are finally bearing fruit. Opponents of neoliberalism are still highly sceptical. It is suggested here that while there are grounds for guarded optimism, deep-seated structural problems remain which will prevent Latin America from matching East Asia's economic dynamism.

Latin America is a large and diverse region. This short study cannot do justice to the great range of variation between particular countries, and therefore concentrates on establishing general themes, sometimes illustrated with national cases. Brazil under its 1964–85 military regime, provides the most conspicuous example of a 'development dictatorship' pursuing ISI and, for a time, apparently enjoying some success with the strategy. Argentina has been noted for its economic retardation, chronic social conflict, and powerful trade union movement. In Chile special domestic circumstances led to unusually vigorous neoliberal measures, perhaps with some useful results. Cuba illustrates the hopes and disappointments of a socialist revolution. There are several excellent books which detail the contrasting histories of individual Latin American countries at greater length (Sheahan 1987; Wynia 1990; Bethell 1991; Williamson 1992; Keen and Haynes 2000; Skidmore and Smith 2001).

Notes

1 The term 'Indian' is employed here for the region's indigenous people, following normal Latin American usage. However, in English-speaking countries the alternatives 'native American', 'indigenous American', or 'Amerindian', are now often preferred.
2 Some definitions of Latin America include Haiti, formerly the French colony of Saint-Domingue. However, this book considers only those territories that were under Spanish or Portuguese rule until the early nineteenth century, excluding Puerto Rico, taken by the US from Spain in 1898. The Dominican Republic finally gained its independence from Spain in 1865; Cuba did so in 1898.

2 Economic development: ISI

We begin by putting the Latin American development record since 1945 in longer term and international context, noting also the experience of particular countries (Tables 1.2, 2.2). Latin America as a whole achieved quite rapid growth in output per head from the 1940s until the early 1980s, followed by a severe recession and a weak recovery, halted in 2001–2. The comparatively strong Latin American performance in the 1940s was due, above all, to the market opportunities created for the region's exports by the Second World War and post-war reconstruction, at a time when military conflict limited productive capacity elsewhere. During the 1950–80 period Latin America's growth rate closely matched the developing country average, running a little below East Asia's and the Middle East's, but above Sub-Saharan Africa's and South Asia's. At this stage, the Latin American disadvantage relative to East Asia is fully accounted for by the latter region's scope for post-war recovery in the 1950s and, after 1960, by the exceptional dynamism of the NICs (represented in Table 2.1 by South Korea). For the time being, most other East Asian countries still pursued versions of ISI and had economic growth similar to Latin America's.

Among the major Latin American countries there were significant differences in economic performance between 1950 and 1980. Argentina and Chile showed the least vigour while Brazil had the highest long-term growth average. Considerable changes have occurred in Latin American economic structure (Table 2.2). The relative importance of industry grew rapidly from the 1930s, a trend that slowed after 1960, and was reversed after 1980. Exports' share of regional output declined after 1930, and made a very slight recovery after 1970, with a modest increase in the contribution coming from manufactured goods. In South Korea, representing the NIC experience, rapid industrialization did not begin until the 1950s. It was

Table 2.1 Annual rates of growth in output per head: Latin America and East Asia, 1950–2002 (%)

	1950–9	1960–9	1970–9	1980–9	1990–9	2000–2
Latin America	2.2	2.4	3.0	−0.7	1.7	−0.3
Argentina	1.1	2.8	1.2	−2.3	2.9	−6.4
Brazil	3.4	2.7	5.5	−0.5	1.3	1.4
Chile	1.2	2.0	0.8	1.1	4.4	1.5
Colombia	1.5	2.2	3.3	1.2	0.4	0.1
Mexico	2.9	3.2	3.8	−0.3	1.6	0.9
Peru	2.9	2.3	1.0	−3.4	2.3	1.5
Venezuela	3.8	2.8	1.1	−1.9	0.0	−5.8
East Asia	3.8	2.2	4.0	4.9	5.1	5.0
South Korea	3.7	5.9	7.7	7.8	5.1	4.1

Sources: Maddison 2001; IMF 2002; Sheahan 1987: 95 (for Venezuela 1950–79).

Table 2.2 Changes in economic structure: Latin America and South Korea, 1930–2000

	Share of GDP (%)				
	Agri- culture	Industry	Services	Exports	Manufactures share of exports (%)
Latin America					
1930[a]	45	15	40	30	n.a.
1960	17	33	50	12	5[b]
1970	13	36	51	13	11
1980	10	36	54	12	19
1990	9	36	55	14	34
2000	8	31	61	18	48
South Korea					
1960	35	20	45	3	59[b]
1970	26	30	44	14	77
1980	14	40	46	34	90
1990	9	43	48	29	94
2000	5	44	51	38	91

Sources: Bulmer-Thomas 1994: 192–5, 226; World Bank 2001b; World Bank 2002: 236–9; World Bank 2003: 241.

Notes:
a The figures for this year are rough estimates.
b Estimate for 1965.

associated, after 1960, by a very marked shift towards manufacturing for export.

Brazil and Mexico are, by a wide margin, Latin America's two largest economies, accounting in 2001 for 52 per cent of its population and 58 per cent of its output. They have reached levels of development slightly above the regional average. Argentina, Uruguay, and Chile, are also relatively prosperous. The poorer countries include Venezuela, Peru, Bolivia, Paraguay, Ecuador, Colombia, and the small Central American republics (see map, p. xi). Although agriculture's share of Latin American output fell sharply after 1930, the sector retained a considerable proportion of the workforce, about 50 per cent in the 1950s, and 25 per cent in the 1980s. Labour productivity in Latin America's agriculture is much lower than in its industry, an important cause of the wide income inequalities that characterize the region (Chapter 5).

The discussion in this and the next chapter considers the trends indicated by Tables 2.1 and 2.2, with particular reference to issues raised in Chapter 1. Why, despite the growing difficulties encountered by ISI during the 1950s, did Latin America not shift to a more export-based economic strategy, as happened in the East Asian NICs? Why, after two further decades of essentially inward-oriented development, did Latin America suffer such a severe crisis of foreign indebtedness during the 1980s? Was excessive government intervention to promote ISI the main cause of Latin America's difficulties? Why has subsequent neoliberal reform in the region had such limited results? To what extent can Latin American problems be blamed on outside forces, as claimed by advocates of dependency theory?

Trade policy: inward versus outward orientation

ISI, a drive for greater economic self-reliance, aimed to replace imports with nationally produced manufactures. This policy was begun by the larger Latin American countries during the 1930s, and adopted in most other parts of the post-colonial Third World (including South Korea and Taiwan) after 1945. It often relied on 'developmental' tariffs: highly protective rates for consumer goods (textiles, clothing, etc.); low rates or free entry for necessary inputs and capital goods (oil, steel, machinery, etc.). The common result with Latin America's ISI pioneers was an initial phase of rapid industrial expansion, as capacity grew in the 'easier' sectors, followed during the 1950s by slowdown and mounting economic strains. Intractable current account balance of payments deficits were a characteristic symptom of such ISI 'exhaustion'. Rising expenditures on imported equipment and raw materials, together with the stagnation of traditional commodity exports, more than offset any savings on the import of consumer goods.

The neoliberal interpretation of these difficulties, and of subsequent events, runs as follows. The newly established industries proved high cost and inefficient, not just through technical inexperience, a weakness that might be remedied with the passage of time, but also because the limited size of national markets prevented factories from working at full capacity or achieving economies of large-scale operation. Excluding foreign competition provided a cover for careless management practices. Developmental tariffs accompanied by investment subsidies encouraged capital intensive production methods, so even the fast growth of industrial ouput created few jobs. Unemployment and income inequality rose.

After running into similar problems South Korea and Taiwan recognized from about 1960 that comprehensive ISI was failing and gave it up. They concentrated, instead, on turning out a more limited range of goods for export, mainly to the developed countries. The policy shift proved a remarkable success. Export sales enabled firms to escape the confines of a small national market, and produce on a more extensive, more efficient scale. The competitive effort needed to win foreign orders improved business standards. Developed-country customers, US department stores, for example, gave their new East Asian suppliers technical assistance. At first, the emphasis was put on simple, labour-intensive products (textiles, clothing, shoes, toys). This minimized the need for costly imported capital goods and took full advantage of low NIC wage costs, ensuring a rapid growth of industrial employment. However, vigorous output expansion and the strong demand for labour soon caused wage rates to rise. Manufacturers responded by moving into more advanced, capital-intensive lines (consumer electronics, chemicals, engineering). Export earnings provided the means to upgrade, by importing equipment and technology from the developed countries. International competition stimulated further improvements in business methods. Thus outward-looking growth continued as a dynamic, self-reinforcing process, with the benefits spread among the population at large, through the job opportunities generated by manufacturing. Rapid, widely diffused income gains strengthened the legitimacy of NIC political regimes and limited social conflict (Balassa *et al.* 1986).

In Latin America, on the other hand, although during the 1960s some countries met crises of ISI exhaustion with attempts at encouraging manufactured exports, for various reasons the shift towards an externally oriented development strategy was less decisive than in South Korea or Taiwan. Export promotion, at least in its early stages, required the strict control of wage levels, to keep the 'cheap labour' advantage. Latin America's political conflict and habits of trade union militancy made this difficult (Chapter 5). Also, the need for radical adjustment seemed less urgent than in the East Asian NICs, because other promising options were available. For the main Latin American republics, with their relatively large populations and abundant natural resources, it was apparently feasible to 'deepen' ISI, by building up national capacity in the more sophisticated capital goods industries, and dispensing with foreign suppliers. Latin American governments had neglected agriculture, so it was thought that greater attention to the sector's problems would be rewarding. Agrarian reform schemes were devised, to take underused land from large estates for sharing out as smaller holdings which, it was hoped, would be farmed more intensively by the new owners. Land reform was intended to increase agricultural output, thus easing inflationary and balance of payments pressures. Income would be distributed less unequally, thus enlarging the domestic market for ISI undertakings, and allowing them to bring underused capacity into full operation. Increasing the number of property owners counteracted the threat of subversion from Cuba. (South Korea and Taiwan had already completed thorough land reforms by the 1960s, and agricultural improvement did not offer large dividends.) Much was expected in Latin America from regional trade agreements between neighbouring countries, which would allow local firms to increase their sales volumes behind a high common external tariff (Bulmer-Thomas 1994: 297–322).

Nevertheless, these partial modifications to Latin American ISI had disappointing results. The new stress on the national manufacture of sophisticated capital goods aggravated problems of industrial inefficiency, limited market size, and reliance on imported inputs. Costly licence fees were required to secure advanced technology. So, the long-term deterioration in Latin America's balance of payments continued. During the 1960s, deficits were covered partly through US government aid or loans, increased in response to the Cuban revolution, and through MNC investment. However, by the end of the decade these sources were becoming insufficient. The MNCs faced growing hostility from nationalist opinion, influenced by dependency theory, while the US was less willing to provide official funds because of its expensive war in Vietnam. At the same time, the evolution of new international banking techniques made 'non-official' loans from developed-country commercial banks more readily available. The volume of such loans grew rapidly after the Organization of Petroleum Exporting Countries (OPEC) raised the price of oil from US$3 to $12 per barrel in 1973–4, and to $30 in 1979. OPEC members deposited much of their revenues to earn interest in First World banks. The recessions caused in the developed countries by the oil shocks limited investment opportunities there, and bankers turned to the Third World, Latin America in particular, as an outlet for surplus funds. Most Latin American countries depended on imported oil, so the sudden increases in its price widened balance of payments deficits. Mexico, Venezuela, and Ecuador benefited as oil exporters, but borrowed heavily on the strength of future income to finance ambitious government spending programmes. Thus, Latin America's external debt grew ten-fold during the 1970s, and exceeded US$300 billion by 1982.

Then Mexico announced that payments on its foreign debt could not be maintained, damaging confidence in other Latin American countries, and drastically curtailing new bank loans. The immediate cause of the debt crisis was the neoliberal 'monetarist' policy adopted by Great Britain and the US, relying on high interest rates to control inflation. Between 1978 and 1982 the average annual interest rates on foreign bank loans doubled. At the same time, world-wide recession cut the demand for Latin American exports, still mainly raw materials. By 1982 service charges on foreign debt absorbed nearly 50 per cent of the region's export earnings, and a drastic reduction of economic activity was necessary to limit the demand for imports (Frieden 1991: 59–66; Bethell 1994a: 200–37; Bulmer-Thomas 1994: 358–65).

The East Asian NICs faced the same international circumstances, but coped with them more easily. Hong Kong and Taiwan had been running large balance of payments surpluses, and so were not indebted. Singapore had drawn in foreign capital through MNC investment rather than bank loans. South Korea had borrowed heavily; relative to national output its debt was greater than Mexico's or Brazil's. But Korea's exports constituted a larger share of output, and they were predominantly manufactures, less severely affected than raw materials by the recession. So the country could increase its foreign exchange earnings to meet the heavier interest payments, without suffering the 'import strangulation' that affected Latin America after 1982 (Table 2.5; Banuri 1991: 66–7; Bulmer-Thomas 1994: 363–409).

Thus, neoliberals argue that East Asia's low-tariff, externally oriented industrialization has proved inherently superior to Latin America's modified ISI of the 1960s and 1970s: more efficient, less vulnerable to external shocks, and a model which other countries should follow. Statists, though now generally accepting that Latin American protection and introversion became excessive, have disputed this thesis on two main counts.

First, among the NICs only Hong Kong and Singapore practised free trade from the start of their export drives. South Korea and Taiwan kept high tariffs until the 1980s. Protection was relaxed gradually, easing firms' adjustment to international competition. The needs of manufacturers that required imported inputs for export production were first met by selective duty rebates rather than comprehensive liberalization. Infant industries had a sheltered home market base from which to develop export sales (Green 1995: 182).

Second, whatever the detail of tariff policy, it has been questioned whether the NIC experience is relevant for much of Latin America. The NICs are relatively small and were relatively poor: in 1965 South Korea's output per head was less than 40 per cent of the Latin American average. So, at that date, the country, with a population of 28 million, had a national output of $37 billion (1990 PPP $s). The corresponding figures for Taiwan were 11 million and $27 billion, for Singapore two million and $5 billion. It was obvious that industry here could only achieve an adequate operating scale through exports. But, for at least the larger Latin American republics, such as Brazil (1965 population 83 million, output $203 billion), Mexico (43 million, $167 billion), or Argentina (22 million, $142 billion) ISI might have been feasible with better management. ISI exhaustion was, perhaps, only inevitable for the smaller republics, such as Uruguay (three million, $13 billion). India and China are cited as successful examples of ISI in big countries (Banuri 1991: 72–4, 91–5, 102–7). Some statists have also predicted that any attempt by the larger Third World countries to pursue industrial exporting with the same intensity as the NICs would be stopped by a defensive First World protectionist backlash (Green 1995: 188).

The first of these points carries some weight. It is certainly the case that the tariff regime in South Korea and Taiwan fell far short of free trade for many years after the launch of export-oriented industrialization. Nevertheless, protectionism here was, on the whole, more moderate than Latin America's. Governments in both countries put pressure on firms to reach international standards of efficiency with credible warnings that tariffs would be lowered in the future, as many statists acknowledge (Hewitt *et al.* 1992: 110–11, 177; Green 1995: 182).

The statists' second line of argument, concerning the potential of the bigger Third World countries for rapid, self-sufficient development, is much less persuasive. India and China do not convincingly demonstrate the value of ISI. During the 1950–80 period India's economic record was mediocre. China showed a little more dynamism, but only on the basis of a massive and wasteful investment effort, imposed by a harsh communist dictatorship. In both countries growth accelerated markedly when they began opening themselves up more to international trade, from the late 1970s. The Brazilian economy is large by Latin American standards; hence its relatively strong performance between 1950 and 1980 (Table 2.1). Yet, Brazil's national output at the start of the period was only a quarter of Great Britain's and a sixteenth of the US's, almost certainly too small for efficient ISI. Forecasts that First World protectionism would block export-oriented industrialization by major Third World countries have proved wrong. Since the 1980s, China has built up huge trade surpluses with the US through the export of labour-intensive manufactures. Nevertheless, Washington tolerates this imbalance, partly for geo-political reasons, partly because major US firms in high-technology sectors (aircraft, etc.) value China as a prosperous market.

However, while inward looking development strategies have evidently been mistaken, it should be noted that the degree of introversion reached by Latin America under ISI was comparatively moderate. Between the mid-1950s and 1980 Latin America's exports rose about three-fold (at constant prices), much less than the NIC's 40-fold growth, but a similar rate of increase to China's, and more than twice that of India. In 1980, foreign trade (exports plus imports) as a share of GDP stood at about 25 per cent for Latin America, less than half the level current before the start of ISI, but still above the Asian average. The corresponding figure was 16 per cent for India and China. Within Latin America it ranged from about 50 per cent for Venezuela and the smallest republics, to 20–25 per cent for Mexico and Brazil, and 10 per cent for Argentina, where autarky had been carried furthest (World Bank 2001b).

Industrial policy

Apart from tariff barriers, another key aspect of ISI was encouragement to manufacturing through direct public sector support, commonly termed industrial policy. The elements of industrial policy include state owned enterprises (SOEs), state subsidies to private firms, preferential ordering from national enterprises by the public sector, official agencies for improving quality standards, and government sponsorship of technical training and research. Direct foreign investment (DFI) undertaken by developed-country firms, if permitted at all, may be subject to detailed control, requiring the use of locally purchased inputs, and the sharing of technology with local partners through joint venture arrangements.

Industrial policy was elaborated in Latin America during the post-1960 phase of modified ISI. The belief took hold that the more novel and sophisticated industries which seemed likely to grow rapidly in the future should be given a high priority. They would nurture advanced skills and stimulate innovation in related sectors. A strong indigenous technical capability would give extra bargaining power in negotiation with First World suppliers of expertise. The foreign exchange cost of royalty payments on licensed technology would be minimized. Attention could be paid to developing production methods appropriate for local circumstances.

Dogmatic neoliberals assert that active industrial policy, under which governments try to 'pick winners', has almost invariably been harmful. State bureaucrats with public funds at their disposal are more likely to be careless in routine management, and to launch over-ambitious, ill-judged schemes than are entrepreneurs who risk their own capital, or executives held to account by shareholders (Balassa *et al.* 1986). There is much evidence from Latin America to support this thesis. For example, after the 1973–4 OPEC oil price shock, Brazil embarked on a heavily subsidized project to manufacture ethanol (industrial alcohol) from sugar cane, replacing imported petroleum as fuel for motor vehicles. The ethanol programme turned out to be grossly uneconomic. Borrowing by deficit-ridden SOEs accounted for much of the growth in Latin America's foreign debt.

According to statists, on the other hand, industrial policy can be useful. They argue that the East Asian NICs relied on public sector initiatives as well as market forces to upgrade from the original low-skill, cheap-labour, 'sweat shop' manufacturing export lines. For example, South Korea's government took over most of the country's banks in the early 1960s and used credit subsidies to foster large, conglomerate business corporations (*chaebols*), privately owned, but established with state support after 1945, and under state guidance (Hewitt *et al.* 1992: 115–16). The *chaebols* were made to compete with each other for market share, executive talent, and official patronage. The Korean state oversaw the *chaebols*' successive moves into the production for export of heavy machinery, motor cars, and computer memory chips. Sometimes, the public sector took a more direct role. Thus, the South Korean steel company POSCO was founded in 1970 with government participation, and soon became one of the world's lowest cost steel producers (World Bank 1987: 71). Government technical leadership has also been important for private sector industry in Taiwan, where small firms are more typical (Gereffi and Wyman 1990: 231–66). In the East Asia NICs, government and state enterprise accounted, up to the 1980s, for as large a share of national output (about 25 per cent) as in Latin America (Hewitt *et al.* 1992: 97–127). Both South Korea and Taiwan kept stricter controls on DFI than those adopted by most Latin American countries, reserving all major industries for 'national champions'.

However, experience shows that successful industrial policy requires high quality government institutions, operating on strictly technocratic lines, well-insulated from private sector special interests. For historical reasons this precondition was met in the NICs but not in Latin America, except perhaps for a time in Chile (Chapter 5). The NIC record suggests also that state participation in manufacturing is most likely to be valuable if it reinforces a vigorous, competitive private sector and is export related. Thus, POSCO achieved scale economies by supplying steel to South Korea's export-oriented ship construction yards. As a contrast, Latin American industrial policy usually aimed at deepening ISI, and so lacked focus. SOEs proliferated, many of them with national monopolies (Bulmer-Thomas 1994: 350–8). Scientific and technical manpower, relatively limited in any case by poor educational provision (Chapter 6), was spread over too wide a range of objectives. Elite interest groups secured wasteful, corrupt allocations of state funds (Chapter 5), for example, through the cheap credit given to estate owners under Brazil's ethanol programme. Latin American military dictatorships favoured industries with a strategic potential: armaments, aircraft, nuclear power. Projects in such fields were likely to be technically overambitious. Often they developed as jealously guarded fiefs, linked to particular branches of the armed forces, poorly coordinated, and detached from civilian industry (Rouquié 1987: 294–302). The bias of Latin

Table 2.3 Public sector investment and efficiency, 1970–80

	Public sector share of total investment 1980 (%)	*Incremental capital output ratio 1970–80*
Latin America	35	4.2
NICs	20	3.0
ASEAN 3	40	3.0
India	45	6.2
China	82	5.9

Source: World Bank 2001b.

American official support to capital-intensive methods held back job creation and, partly as a result, the share of the region's labour force employed in industry reached only about 25 per cent by the 1980s, compared to 35 per cent in the NICs.

Nevertheless, as with trade policy, while Latin American industrial policy was inferior to that of the NICs, it does not seem especially damaging when put in wider perspective. Data for the Third World as a whole (Table 2.3) confirm the neoliberal view that a leading public sector economic role during the later ISI period was often associated with the unproductive use of capital. However, in Latin America this role was comparatively modest, and investment efficiency stood relatively high. (The incremental capital output ration, investment's percentage share of GDP, divided by the annual GDP growth rate, roughly measures investment efficiency. The lower the ratio, the less capital is required to generate extra output, and the higher is the efficiency level.)

Large foreign firms have been conspicuous in Latin America. Originally, foreign investment was concentrated in primary export sectors (for example, sugar plantations, or mining), and in infrastructure (railways, electricity supply, telephone services). After 1945 it focused more on manufacturing industry, with governments often actively encouraging foreign participation to help ISI. At the same time, nationalist measures cut back foreign control of landed estates, mining, and utilities. By the 1970s, multinational corporations accounted for about 30 per cent of Latin American manufacturing output. Statists contrast this unfavourably with the more restrictive East and South Asian DFI regimes which, it is claimed, made possible healthier patterns of economic development and more indigenous technical capability. In South Korea and Taiwan the MNCs were allowed to take only a 10 per cent share of industrial output, though the proportion reached 50 per cent in Singapore. DFI was excluded almost entirely from India and China during the ISI period. Some commentators see foreign investment's relative strength in Latin America as an aspect of dependency and a quasi-imperialist intrusion (Green 1991: 11–14, 69). Most MNC investment has come from the US, although since the 1960s many European and Japanese firms have entered the region.

It is suggested that MNC penetration has had many damaging consequences for Latin America. The MNCs' control of advanced technology allowed them to exercise monopoly power, and take out large profits, at the expense of the host countries' balance of payments (Skidmore and Smith 2001: 383). The MNCs have been reluctant to produce for export from their Latin American operations, in competition with parent companies' plants elsewhere. The MNCs tended to operate as isolated enclaves, making little use of local suppliers, and preferring capital-intensive methods that require only a small work force. In certain sectors, for example the pharmaceutical industry, MNCs acquired or displaced locally owned firms which had quite high levels of technical expertise. The subsidiaries then gave up research and development work, to concentrate instead on routine manufacturing.

Most of these points are open to question. First, the MNCs on the whole did not force themselves into Latin America. They usually invested as a result of measures designed to attract them by national governments, so any harm that followed can be seen more as the expression of weaknesses internal to the region, rather than as an external imposition. For example, Brazil's MNC-controlled automobile assembly industry was established in the 1950s despite technical studies which showed that the country would have benefited from a greater emphasis on railways. However, railway improvement, or the establishment of a state-owned automobile firm as a 'national champion', required heavy government spending, and the taxes to pay for this could not be raised because of domestic political difficulties (Shapiro 1994: 28–69).

Second, although it is true that during the early years of their Latin American operations in the 1950s and 1960s MNC manufacturing enterprises often did make unreasonably high profits, while failing to purchase local supplies, or to share technology, with the passage of time these faults were recognized. As host governments built up the necessary expertise, they bargained more forcefully, at least in the larger republics, imposing more stringent rules on foreign firms concerning import content and other matters (Bennett and Sharpe 1985). Often these rules became tighter than those applied in East Asia. New investments were increasingly confined to joint ventures with local capital, as under Brazil's *tri-pé* system of three-way partnership between MNCs, state enterprises, and private sector national firms (Evans 1979).

Third, it is unlikely that an ingrained reluctance on the part of the MNCs to export from their subsidiaries seriously weakened Latin America's balance of payments or aggravated the region's foreign indebtedness. From the 1960s competitive pressures began encouraging MNCs to supply much of their global business through operations in developing countries, where labour costs are relatively low. MNC branch plants in East Asia have been export-oriented, useful earners of foreign exchange for their host countries', despite profit remittances. It was local circumstances – overvalued currencies (see below), political uncertainty, poor infrastructure, the weak implementation of industrial support programmes – that did most to prevent the MNCs from playing a similar role in Latin America. Even here MNC manufacturing enterprises came by the 1970s to export a greater proportion of their output than did national firms (Haggard 1990: 218). Productivity growth accelerated in China and India after 1980 when foreign investors were admitted more freely. On balance, it is likely that the latitude allowed to DFI during the ISI period was a cause of the region's relatively low incremental capital output ratio.

Macroeconomics: inflation, budget deficits, savings, and foreign debt

Latin America since 1945 has been clearly distinctive for its persistent macroeconomic instability and unusually rapid price inflation (Table 2.4). However, the record differs widely between countries within the region. During the 1950–80 period, high inflation was a particular phenomenon of the larger or wealthier republics which had been pursuing ISI since the 1930s. Inflation averaged 67 per cent a year in the Southern Cone, and 34 per cent in Brazil, though only 9 per cent in Mexico and 13 per cent in Colombia. As a contrast, the average was about 5 per cent in Central America, for example, where ISI did not begin until the 1960s.

Neoliberals argue that rapid inflation does considerable harm, by discouraging productive investment and by aggravating business uncertainty. The price level in Latin American countries has often

Table 2.4 Price inflation: annual average rates, 1950–2002 (%)

	1950–9	1960–9	1970–9	1980–9	1990–4	1995–9	2000–2
Latin America	17	26	35	134	225	18	8.0
NICs	22	8	14	5	7	2	–0.2
South Korea	37	14	20	7	8	3	0.5
India	2	9	8	8	10	9	4.0
China	n.d.	1	2	6	10	5	0.2
Developed countries	3	3	8	6	4	2	1.4

Sources: World Bank 1984b, 2001b; IMF 1998, 2002; Thorp 1998: 332.

risen rapidly, without appropriate adjustments to foreign exchange rates. Currencies have thus become overvalued, making the region's exports uncompetitive in world markets. Increases in the real effective exchange rate (REER: see Glossary) have limited the development of export sales. Therefore a high priority should be given to establishing price stability, the neglect of which, neoliberals allege, has been a main cause of Latin America's economic difficulties.

Statists have tried to dispute this emphasis. A favourite theme of ECLA structuralism, elaborated in response to IMF-prescribed austerity programmes from the late 1950s, was that inflation should be seen as a symptom of more fundamental weaknesses. They included elite opposition to higher taxes, and the failure of archaic estate agriculture to produce sufficient food for rapidly growing urban populations. Until these difficulties could be overcome, then inflation should be accepted as a price worth paying to achieve development. More recent critics of neoliberalism cite instances where a country's exports have grown strongly, despite an appreciating REER (Banuri 1991: 86–8). Such arguments are unconvincing. On causes, the structuralist thesis relating to food supply is contradicted by Argentina and Uruguay, which had high inflation despite their unusually productive agriculture. On consequences, it is certainly true that the relationship between inflation and economic performance is not exact: for example, within Latin America until the 1980s Brazil had the region's highest rate of output growth, and also relatively high inflation. Among the NICs, South Korea had a rather poor record on price stability between 1950 and 1980 (Table 2.4). But there can be no doubt that the very severe inflation which became common after the 1982 debt crisis in Latin America, as a legacy of previous trends, made recovery more difficult (Chapter 3), and that over the longer term Latin American exporters have been disadvantaged by REER instability (Morawetz 1981: 39–55; Lin 1989, 176–82; Bulmer-Thomas 1994: 352–3, 380–1).

Latin American inflation resulted partly from the effect of the Second World War period shortages in pushing up price levels, and from the extra protection given under ISI to high-cost, monopolistic national industries. However, other developing regions also experienced such forces yet coped with them more effectively, so attention must focus on other influences. Above all, the political weakness of Latin America's populist governments (Chapter 5) limited their ability to impose new taxes or contain pressures for extra spending. State revenues lagged behind the growth of public sector expenditure, and budget deficits were financed by enlarging the money supply. In the Southern Cone republics, heavily urbanized and with powerful labour movements, severe strains on public finances came from the demands of government employees and unionized industrial workers for higher pay. At an early stage of ISI these countries also had quite extensive and costly social welfare programmes (Chapter 6). Brazil was less urbanized, with more limited popular mobilization, but here powerful business elites secured cheap credit and lavish public sector investment outlays. In Mexico and Colombia dominant party regimes could impose somewhat greater financial restraint. Mexico's distinctive 'stabilizing development' brought annual inflation down to only 3 per cent in the late 1950s, though growing social tensions made this policy unravel after 1970.

The common pattern in the more advanced Latin American countries was for inflation to run at relatively high levels by world standards, so exports became uncompetitive. One possible response was a devaluation of the national currency. However, post-1945 governments were reluctant to devalue, because doing so benefited traditional export interests (large landowners, foreign mining companies), and made manufacturers' imported inputs more expensive. Indeed, populist policy saw overvaluation as a convenient way of taxing exporters to subsidize ISI. Devaluation was usually postponed until balance of payments difficulties made it unavoidable as a crisis measure, which then aggravated inflation by suddenly raising the cost of essential imports (Bulmer-Thomas 1994: 251–5, 283–7).

Inflationary expectations became so firmly established that they could not be broken even by the more authoritarian regimes that came to power after 1960. For example, Brazil's military dictatorship accommodated inflation by frequent small 'crawling peg' devaluations to maintain export competitiveness. However, during the 1970s Brazil and several of its neighbours tried unsuccessfully to cushion

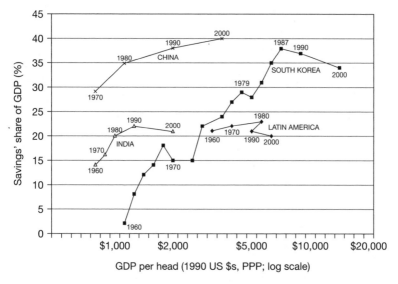

Figure 2.1 Savings relative to GDP per head, 1960–2000
Sources: World Bank 2001b, 2002; Maddison 2001.

the impact from the OPEC oil price increases by limiting further devaluation. REERs therefore rose and exports were discouraged.

Latin America's macroeconomic weakness had other aspects. By international standards the savings rate as a share of GDP was very low for such 'middle income' countries (Figure 2.1). National savings include three components: savings by government, by business enterprises (through profits), and by individuals or households. We have already noticed the influences encouraging Latin American government consumption outlays at the expense of savings and investment. Private sector business profitability in the region seems, on the whole, to have been quite high, except sometimes where nationalist measures burdened foreign firms. However, personal or household savings were comparatively low, for reasons which have yet to be fully clarified. It is commonly believed that rapid income growth favours a high savings rate, because consumption habits often tend to lag behind rising prosperity. Yet, savings stagnated in Brazil, even during periods of vigorous economic advance, just as in the less dynamic Southern Cone. Another possibility is that persistent high inflation encouraged spending on physical assets (houses, cars, jewellery, etc.), to hedge against the declining value of money. Yet, savings remained low in Mexico during its phase of moderate inflation, and in post-1964 Brazil when the military regime established the indexation of government bonds and other financial instruments to compensate for rising prices. Some authors believe that Latin America's state pension schemes discouraged individuals from saving for their old age (Chapter 6). Finally, alleged cultural influences attract a good deal of notice. Latin American upper and middle classes, it is argued, have been particularly eager to imitate affluent First World life styles. The strength of such a 'demonstration effect' may come from the colonial background, from the elites' wish to affirm status in highly unequal societies, and from the close proximity of the US (Orlove 1997). Much MNC investment under ISI was dedicated to the supply of consumer durables such as motor cars. The MNCs' advertising campaigns perhaps encouraged spending and limited personal savings.

These macroeconomic weaknesses provided the context for the rapid growth of Latin America's foreign debt charges in the late 1970s and early 1980s (Table 2.5).

The region's investment rate, though quite modest by international standards, exceeded the savings rate, requiring a large net resource inflow. Elsewhere, in India and Sub-Saharan Africa for example, there were similar funding gaps, but they could be covered to a large extent by development aid from the First World and the Soviet Union. Latin America, on the other hand, was thought fairly prosperous and of lesser strategic importance. So the region attracted little foreign aid and had to rely instead on commercial bank loans. Their cost rose sharply with higher First World interest rates during the 1978–82 period. Finally, many Latin American countries suffered large-scale capital flight because of political uncertainties (Chapter 5), and

Table 2.5 Interest payments on foreign debt as a proportion of exports, 1970–2000 (%)

	1970	*1980*	*1982*	*1990*	*2000*
Latin America	9	19	30	12	11
Argentina	19	21	37	16	30
Brazil	8	34	49	6	22
Chile	8	19	46	17	9
Mexico	24	25	40	13	7
South Korea	9	13	15	3	3
India	8	4	7	19	5
China	0	2	3	5	3

Sources: World Bank 1989b, 2002b.

because accelerating inflation made exchange rates overvalued to an obviously unsustainable degree. Funds were shifted into foreign currency holdings abroad as an insurance against devaluation losses. Much of the increase in Latin America's external debt came through public sector borrowing to counterbalance the outflow of private sector wealth (Edwards 1995: 17–23).

Conclusion

To sum up so far, it is clear that ISI, combining high levels of tariff protection with a large public sector industrial role, as practised in Latin America and most other parts of the Third World during the 1945–80 period, was less effective than the outward-looking development stance adopted by the NICs. However, Latin American forms of trade and industrial policy do not, on the whole, appear unusually extreme or mismanaged. The region's particular problems derived mainly from an insufficient fiscal effort and lax monetary control.

Certain Latin American weaknesses were, above all, domestic in origin, for example inflation, REER instability, the choice of trade policy, and the maladministration of industrial policy. Investment by MNCs probably raised business standards and to that extent did not constitute a damaging external imposition, though it possibly encouraged consumerism at the expense of personal savings. However, other difficulties may perhaps be seen more plainly as the result of unfavourable international circumstances. The immediate cause of the 1982 debt crisis was the sudden rise in interest rates generated by the developed countries' turn to 'monetarist' economics. Subsequently, Latin America would be heavily burdened by the service charges on its foreign loans. Some authors claim that the MNCs had a disruptive political effect in their host countries. The next three chapters will consider further the role of internal and external forces as influences on the region.

3 Economic development
Neoliberal reform

Neoliberal policies were adopted widely across Latin America between the 1970s and early 1990s. When countries took this course they often did so through abrupt and sweeping reversals of ISI, unlike the more gradual approach to free market adjustment taken in East and South Asia. For example, decisive policy shifts occurred over just a few years in Chile (1973–9), Mexico (1985–90), and Peru (1990–2), while in China reform began during the late 1970s, but on certain points is still far from complete.

The neoliberal agenda for Latin America had five main components. The first was a determined effort to achieve low inflation with balanced government budgets. Second, protective barriers against imports were swept away, and exporting became a central objective. Third, the public sector reduced its role in production by selling off or closing down SOEs. Fourth, direct foreign investment was freed from restrictions and actively encouraged. Fifth, financial liberalization deregulated domestic banking and cross-border capital movements. These various aspects of reform were distinct, but seen by their advocates as interrelated and mutually reinforcing. For example, it was hoped that greater competition from imported goods would help to bring down inflation, while the sale of state enterprises would strengthen government finances.

Latin America's neoliberal reforms have had very mixed results. Perhaps the clearest achievement is lower inflation (Table 2.4). Budget deficits narrowed, at least for a time, in the early 1990s. The region has attracted very considerable DFI inflows, occurring on a much larger scale relative to population and GDP than in most other parts of the Third World. However, Latin America's domestic investment and savings effort remains comparatively weak (Figure 2.1). Export orientation has risen only slightly since 1980 and still falls far short of East Asian NIC levels; industry's share of output has declined (Table 2.2). The record of output growth is mediocre. Latin America experienced severe recession for much of the 1980s after the almost complete halt to new foreign bank lending. A modest post-1990 economic revival brought an import surge and widening current account deficits, covered by the resumption of large-scale capital inflows. But the region proved vulnerable once again when outside funding became more difficult to secure and world commodity markets deteriorated as a result of financial crises in East Asia and Russia during the late 1990s (Table 2.1; Figure 3.1). All this contrasts with the NICs' successful pursuit of export-led growth from the 1960s, and with the gains made by the second wave of Asian recruits to a more outward-looking development style from the 1980s.

Why has Latin America's recent progress been so slight? Early neoliberal analysis stressed, above all, the deep-seated macroeconomic weaknesses built up under ISI: chronic inflation, wide budget deficits, and wasteful, inefficient state industries (Balassa *et al.* 1986). So, free market reform should focus on correcting these problems. The results might be painful and disappointing over the short term, but there was no credible policy alternative. From about 1990 rising popular hostility to reform measures in Latin America made neoliberals supplement their emphasis on macroeconomic stabilization

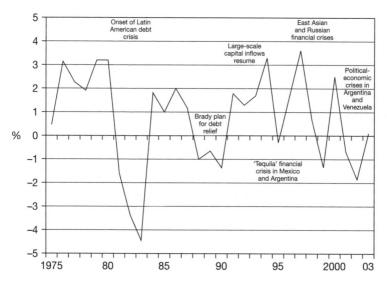

Figure 3.1 Output per head growth in Latin America, 1975–2003*
(% change on a year earlier)

Sources: Maddison 2001; IMF 2002. Note: *Forecast estimate for 2003.

with a greater concern to improve social welfare and lessen the extreme income inequality that marks the region. These latter points, it was claimed, could be addressed within the neoliberal framework through carefully targeted social services and policies to maximize job creation (Edwards 1995).

Statists agree that the legacy of ISI was poor, but differ from the neoliberals in diagnosis and emphasis (Green 1995; Huddle 1997). They have little faith in the possibilities for combining social progress with free market doctrine, and attach great importance to Latin America's unfavourable international circumstances, especially its foreign debt. (Neoliberals acknowledge the debt burden, but rather discount it by noting the concessions that creditors made available.) Among statists there are various shades of opinion. The severest critics from the radical left claim that the whole neoliberal approach is pernicious: foisted on Latin America by the US government in collusion with the IMF and World Bank, to serve a narrow range of business interests. The hardships and flagrant inequity of the new economic model are provoking grassroots reactions, for example the Chiapas uprising in Mexico (1994–) or the election as president of the militant populist Hugo Chávez in Venezuela (1998) which, sooner or later, will bring a complete change of direction (Keen and Haynes 2000: 305–10, 517–22, 578–81). Neo-structuralists, on the other hand, take a more qualified position. While sharing the neoliberal concern for fiscal restraint, and conceding that free market reform has brought some benefit, they believe that the new economic model is showing faults which can only be corrected if the state resumes a more active development role (Stallings and Peres 2000).

Here, we discuss these issues, looking both at overall Latin American trends and at particular national records. The timing of reform differed between countries. Chile embarked on the process in 1973. Argentina, Uruguay, and Peru also began to change course in the 1970s, but their early experiments were not sustained. Mexico, Bolivia, Ecuador, and some Central American republics took liberalizing initiatives in the mid-1980s, soon after the debt crisis had broken. A declared commitment to free market strategies became general in the region by the end of the decade, through their apparent success in Chile, the poor results from attempts at reviving state-led development elsewhere, the growing influence of the Washington financial institutions, and the collapse of Eastern Europe's communist regimes.

Once started, the application of neoliberal doctrine was more thorough in some cases than in others. Reform went furthest in Chile,

Mexico, El Salvador, Argentina (from 1989), and Peru (from 1990). Brazil, Colombia, and Costa Rica were more cautious and qualified converts. Ambitious reform schemes began in Uruguay, Bolivia, Ecuador, and Venezuela, but then lost momentum. Paraguay never showed much warmth for neoliberalism. Cuba explicitly reaffirmed its socialist stance in the mid-1990s. This variety was the result of distinctive national politics, to be considered later (Chapter 5). The present chapter focuses as far as possible on the economic measures taken and their economic effects.

Only Chile, the free-market pioneer, stands out from the general Latin American pattern of very limited gains in output per head since 1980, with a performance notably stronger than the regional average and an improvement on the ISI period, at least during the 1990s. So Chile is taken by some as evidence for the benefits of energetic neoliberalism. However, the country's growth rate fell back below the East Asian and developing country average at the turn of the century (Tables 1.2, 2.1). Mexico, Peru, and El Salvador (aggressive reformers), and Brazil (cautious reformer) have made some progress since the early 1990s, though at a slow pace by pre-1980 standards. But Colombia (cautious reformer) lost the resilience which it had shown during the 1980s, while Argentina (aggressive reformer) continued a pattern of instability, with recovery in the 1990s followed by a crisis in 2001–2 that impacted severely on adjacent Uruguay. Venezuela, Ecuador, Bolivia (interrupted reformers), Paraguay, and Cuba (non-reformers) suffered almost continuous economic stagnation or decline.

On the whole, therefore, the most thorough reform efforts seem to have brought the most rapid growth, but there are numerous exceptions, and many other reasons why argument by association for the benefits of neoliberalism cannot be pushed far. Detailed research on the effect of particular measures has only just begun to appear. Evaluating the 'strength' of reform is debatable. How do we categorize Brazil, where there was extensive privatization but also persistent fiscal deficits, or Costa Rica, with little privatization but a quite vigorous manufacturing export drive? In countries where neoliberal programmes aborted or never really began, this was, as a rule, the effect of political weakness and confusion, rather than a clear commitment to some statist course (except perhaps for Uruguay and Cuba). Finally, there are difficult judgements to make concerning the likely trade-off between policy alternatives. For example, how far could a government safely go in cutting expenditure to correct a budget deficit, when austerity might provoke unmanageable social

Table 3.1 Economic liberalization in South Korea, 1960–80, and Latin America, 1980–2002

	(1)	(2)	(3)	(4)	(5)	(6)	(7)	(8)	(9)	(10)	(11)	(12)	(13)	(14)	(15)	(16)
	1990–2002	1985	1980–9 2001	1990–2001	1990–2000	2000	1990–9 2002	1990–8 1990–9 1998	1990–9 1998	1990–9 2001	1990–9	1990–9 1990–90	1990–9	1990–9 1985–90	1990–7 1990–9	1990–9

A Latin American countries with per capita GDP growth above the regional average, 1990–2002

	(1)	(2)	(3)	(4)	(5)	(6)	(7)	(8)	(9)	(10)	(11)	(12)	(13)	(14)	(15)	(16)
Chile	3.7	39	21	7	9.7	16	−10	4.0	12	25	25	0	−5	0.52	61	37
Dominican Rep.	3.5	29	22	9	n.d.	77^d	+12	1.1	22	22	14	−8	+2	n.d.	n.d.	24
El Salvador	2.2	23	1	7	13.1	48	+52	0.2	23	17	3	−14	+3	n.d.	n.d.	35
Peru	2.1	22	220	23	9.9	20	−3	1.4	16	21	18	−3	+2	0.52	85	28
Panama	1.7	50	5	2	9.7	16	+58	3.5	17	27	25	−2	+3	n.d.	n.d.	23
Costa Rica	1.6	45	24	16	17.2	66	+44	1.5	23	20	17	−3	+3	0.42	24	20
Mexico	1.4	24	72	18	15.9	83	−12	1.2	8	23	21	−2	0	0.48	24	19
Brazil	1.3	19	284	16^e	9.0	59	+75	1.1	17	21	20	−1	−2	0.62	19	33
Guatemala	1.2	13	15	10	11.0	32	+28	1.4	13	16	9	−7	−2	n.d.	n.d.	29

B Latin American countries with per capita GDP growth below the regional average, 1990–2002

	(1)	(2)	(3)	(4)	(5)	(6)	(7)	(8)	(9)	(10)	(11)	(12)	(13)	(14)	(15)	(16)
Argentina	0.8	29	391	4	11.7	32	+11	1.9	9	18	17	−1	−3	0.46	28	28
Bolivia	0.6	44	327	8	4.2	29	−4	2.3	34	17	10	−7	−2	0.48	116	26
Nicaragua	0.4	111	422	39^f	14.3	8	−14	0.9	32	26	−6	−32	−10	n.d.	n.d.	33
Honduras	0.3	42	6	18	8.7	33	+46	0.6	28	31	23	−8	−1	n.d.	n.d.	32

	1960–79	1970	1950–9	1960–79	1960–79	1980	1970–80	1976–80	1980	1960–79	1960–79	1960–79	1970–9	1965	1970–9	1970–80
Colombia	0.3	13	25	20	7.5	34	+11	1.0	40	20	18	−2	−13	0.47	116	23
Uruguay	0.2	28	63	28	6.1	42	+3	0.4	29	15	16	+1	−4	0.45	n.d.	29
Ecuador	0.2	28	36	39	6.6	10	−29	1.3	30	19	22	+3	+1	n.d.	n.d.	38
Paraguay	−1.1	18	24	12	1.7	19	+30	0.7	35	23	10	−13	−8	n.d.	n.d.	23
Venezuela	−1.3	29	19	43	2.2[g]	9	−42	2.0	46	18	24	+6	−7	0.39	n.d.	20
Cuba	−3.0[g]	n.d.	n.d.	n.d.	−9.7	n.d.	+6	n.d.	n.d.	n.d.	n.d.	n.d.	n.d.	n.d.	n.d.	36
Unweighted averages																
Group A	2.1	29	22[h]	10[h]	11.9	46	+27	1.7	17	21	17	−4	0	0.51	43	25
Group B	−0.3	38	63[h]	20[h]	5.3	24	+2	1.2	31	21	15	−6	−5	0.45	87	29
C South Korea	6.8	12	37	17	27.0	90	−38	0.1	14	23	15	−8	+14	0.34	n.d.	32

Sources: (1) as for Table 2.1; (2) debt figures from World Bank 1989b and 2002b combined with PPP GDP estimates from Maddison 2001; (3)–(4) as for Table 2.3; (5), (7)–(13), (16) World Bank 2001b; (6) World Bank 2003: 240–1; (14) Thorp 1998: 352, Stallings and Peres 2000: 130, Pscharapoulos 1991: 19; (15) Stallings and Peres 2000: 66.

Notes: a The excess of investment (10) over savings (11); b The higher the number, the greater the level of inequality; c Mortality of children aged 0–1 year; d 1996; e 1995–2001; f 1990–9; g 1990–8; h median.

Key to columns: (1) Annual growth of per capita GDP (%); (2) Foreign debt as a % of GDP (%); (3), (4) Annual inflation (%); (5) Annual growth of exports (%); (6) Manufactures' share of exports (%); (7) Change in terms of trade (%); (8) DFI as a % of GDP (%); (9) Public sector share of investment (%); (10) Investment as a % of GDP; (11) Savings as a % of GDP; (12) Net inward (−) or outward (+) resource transfer[a] as a % of GDP; (13) Change in savings' % share of GDP; (14) Gini index[b] of income inequality; (15) Increase in government social spending per head; (16) Decrease in infant mortality[c] (%)

conflict? Local circumstances make the probable answer differ from country to country. Neoliberal economics were often adopted soon after a change from military dictatorship to civilian democracy. However, in Chile, military rule lasted until 1989 and Mexico kept its dominant party system until the late 1990s.

Argentina and Venezuela require particular attention, because their recent crises account for three quarters of the slowdown in Latin America's economic growth during the 2000–2 period. Do these republics prefigure wider convulsions and the final bankruptcy of neoliberalism forecast by the left? Or is it more likely that they are special cases and will give neighbours a salutary warning of mistakes to avoid?

To support our assessment Table 3.1 presents economic and social indicators for each Latin American country since the onset of liberalization. The countries are ranked according to their rate of increase in output per head since 1990, with a division between those making above-average advances, generously termed 'fast growers' (Group A), and the below-average 'slow growers' (Group B). This layout may suggest whether or not a particular variable is likely to have had a major effect on economic performance. The table includes comparable data for South Korea during the 1950–80 period, and uses group medians or simple averages (unweighted by size of output or population), so that the large countries' experience does not overwhelm that of the smaller.

Macroeconomic management: budget deficits and inflation

Latin American ISI had entailed large fiscal deficits and chronic inflation. Tackling these imbalances came to be seen as an urgent matter, in some cases long before other neoliberal recommendations were accepted. The onset of the debt crisis in the early 1980s widened deficits by increasing the interest and repayment charges due on foreign loans, typically from about 10 per cent to about 30 per cent of government expenditure, just when economic recession was depressing tax yields and state enterprise profits. Falling exchange rates raised the national currency cost of foreign debt service; revenue shortfalls were covered by printing money and by domestic borrowing at very high rates of interest. This created vicious circles of currency depreciation and budgetary weakness. Shifts from authoritarian rule to democracy allowed organized labour more freedom to force up wage rates, giving the inflationary spiral an extra twist. Latin

America's public sector budget deficits averaged about 3 per cent of GDP in the 1970s and 7 per cent in the 1980s. For comparison, NIC deficits rarely exceeded 1–2 per cent of GDP. Latin American inflation averaged 35 per cent a year in the 1970s and 134 per cent in the 1980s. Corresponding figures for the East Asian NICs are 14 per cent and 5 per cent (Table 2.4).

Certain Latin American countries suffered especially severe upsurges of inflation. For example, by 1989–90 the annual rate of price increase had reached 3,000 per cent in Brazil and Argentina, and 8,000 per cent in Peru. These episodes resulted from democratic pressures and the failure of 'heterodox' attempts at checking inflation without austerity measures to limit consumption. However, Mexico's dominant party regime held average yearly inflation down to 70 per cent in the 1980s, only four times the average of the previous decade. Chile's military dictatorship cut inflation from a 1973 peak of 600 per cent to an average 20 per cent in the 1980s. A more general stabilization came in the early 1990s, partly through changing public attitudes where prices seemed to be running completely out of control. In Argentina, Brazil, and Peru, fear of hyperinflation let elected politicians implement more decisive adjustment programmes. At the same time the Brady plan, a US-backed scheme for debt relief linked to neoliberal reform (Chapter 4), gave Latin American governments a means of cutting down their service charges. The burden of interest payments fell (Table 2.5). Deficit reduction came also through selling off state enterprises, a course often prescribed under Brady plan deals. There were more determined efforts to increase tax collection. Renewed capital inflows supported exchange rates. Virtuous circles of currency stabilization, falling interest rates, and strengthening public finances, replaced the self-reinforcing crises of the previous decade.

For a time after 1990 many Latin American governments had balanced budgets, and average inflation was reduced sharply, though it still remained quite high by developed country standards (Table 2.4). Central banks were given greater autonomy, reinforcing the impression of monetary discipline. Argentina set its currency, by law, at what was declared to be an unalterable parity with the US dollar. Other countries relied on crawling peg mechanisms: frequent pre-announced mini-devaluations below the current rate of inflation, providing an exchange rate 'anchor' to help achieve price stability. However, the slowing down of inflation lagged well behind currency stabilization, so REERs often increased considerably. Furthermore, government budget deficits soon reappeared, most notably in Brazil, where a new democratic constitution had combined a large increase of public sector payrolls and pension rights with looser central control over state and municipal administrations. A few countries, in particular Mexico and Chile, kept a relatively austere fiscal stance.

Statists accept that the extreme post-1982 macroeconomic turbulence had to be corrected, but sometimes imply that because it resulted, above all, from 'unjust' foreign debt, Latin American governments should have been bolder in claiming relief, and creditors should have been more forgiving (Green 1991: 72–80; Huddle 1997: 892–3). Most countries fell behind in their debt service payments, but only Cuba declared a full default during the 1980s. Ethical issues lie beyond the scope of this study. We can only note that, rightly or wrongly, First World commercial banks lending to Latin America sought a market rate of return, and when disappointed could exact a heavy price, though self-interest eventually made them offer some debt forgiveness under the Brady plan (Chapter 4). Those countries that conformed most closely to neoliberal ideas of financial rectitude would get an improved credit rating. In any case, while Latin America's debt burden in the 1980s was certainly heavier than that of the NICs when they embarked on export-oriented industrialization, and no doubt disadvantageous, differences between countries in the region on this point are weakly correlated with GDP growth, suggesting that indebtedness by itself did not act as a decisive influence (Table 3.1, column 2). The ability to bring down inflation by the 1990s seems more important, though the cases of Argentina and Bolivia show that improved price stability did not guarantee economic success (Table 3.1, columns 3 and 4).

Statists argue, further, that more should have been done to defend social welfare provision from budget cuts, and to increase government revenue from direct taxes on upper-class incomes, rather than from the higher sales taxes and utility charges falling largely on the poor that became the staple of fiscal adjustment. But, in fact, social spending did not lose out as much as other categories. Its share of total public outlays stood at 40 per cent (11 per cent of GDP) in 1980–1, 42 per cent (10 per cent of GDP) in 1990–1, and 49 per cent (13 per cent of GDP) in 1996–7 (Stallings and Peres 2000: 66). Public sector investment and business subsidies suffered the largest cuts. Extra social spending was a main cause of rising Latin American budget deficits during the 1990s. The resources committed were modest by developed-country standards, but higher as a share of GDP than anywhere else in the Third World, a legacy from populist Latin American ISI (Chapter 6). The failure to make significant increases in direct taxation resulted, above all, from opposition by national elites. The World Bank and other sources of neoliberal advice urged that more action be taken on this point (Edwards 1995: 313). Levels of income inequality in Latin America had little bearing on national prospects for economic recovery (Table 3.1, column 14). Also, those countries which showed an above-average commitment to improving welfare, measured by increases in government social spending and decreases in infant mortality, were not, on the whole, rewarded with particularly rapid output per head growth (Table 3.1, columns 15 and 16), though of course welfare gains may be considered desirable for their own sake.

Both statists and neoliberals agree that the sudden capital inflows and REER appreciations which often supported adjustment had undesirable side effects (see below). However, it is doubtful in most cases whether inflation could have been checked by any other means. The failure of heterodox stabilization programmes suggests that the only viable alternative was harsh austerity, as implemented by the 1973–89 Chilean military regime, not an option for emerging democracies or quasi-democracies elsewhere.

Turning to Asian comparisons, in South Korea and Taiwan episodes of hyperinflation during the immediate post-1945 period had convinced policy makers of the need for financial restraint, and strong authoritarian governments could put their views into effect. The shift away from ISI during the 1960s occurred against a background of relative price stability, quite unlike Latin America in the 1980s. The inflationary effects from the devaluations that launched the East Asian NICs' export drives were easily contained. Thereafter, the basic resilience of the growth process assured financial equilibrium (Lin 1991: 128–90). Governments made a substantial contribution to the growth of national savings, in a way that has not proved possible for Latin America (Edwards 1995: 224–43). In China and India liberalization was accompanied by large public sector deficits, but they could be managed without undue difficulty, thanks to relatively high domestic private sector savings, strong financial systems, and modest levels of foreign debt.

Tariff and industrial policy

Neoliberal policy in Latin America brought the rapid dismantling of protective tariff barriers and other state support for industry. For example, between 1973 and 1979 Chile eliminated import quotas, and cut the average duty from about 100 per cent to 10 per cent. By the early 1990s most other countries had followed suit. Commercial liberalization was reinforced by establishing regional customs unions, most notably the North American Free Trade Agreement (NAFTA), concluded between the US, Canada, and Mexico in 1993, and *Mercosur* linking Brazil, Argentina, Uruguay, and Paraguay in 1991. Chile's post-1973 military rulers, following their overthrow of the radical Allende government, undertook a rapid tariff liberalization because they believed that ISI had fostered collectivist mentalities and allowed a communist-led labour movement, nurtured by an over-protected manufacturing sector, to gain power. It was felt necessary to cleanse society of these influences as quickly as possible. Military regimes in the other Southern Cone countries took a similar course, influenced by a similar doctrinaire revulsion against the threat from the radical left (Frieden 1991: 155–8, 206–11). From 1982, foreign creditors had more influence; they often made immediate tariff cuts a condition for debt rescheduling. The Washington consensus held that liberalization should be rapid, both to help curb inflation and to ensure that the reform process was sustained. The vested interests associated with the old protective system should be allowed no time to regroup and reassert themselves (World Bank 1987: 100, 108–10). All this contrasts with East Asia and India where, in most cases, the dismantling of tariff barriers came gradually over periods of twenty or thirty years.

At the same time as they undertook trade liberalization, Latin American countries cut their public sector investment and began the privatization of state enterprises. In post-1973 Chile and, to a lesser extent, Mexico from 1985, divestitures were a reaction against leftist initiatives which had extended the state's economic role during the last stages of ISI, but across the region as a whole the overriding influence was financial. The sale of SOEs offered a means to cut budget deficits and foreign debt. Over the last three decades Latin America has accounted for 60–70 per cent of privatization income in the developing world. Relative to GDP Latin America's privatization revenues have been five times larger than East Asia's (World Bank 2001b: 14, 270–2). A large proportion of the assets sold off were utilities (for example, electric power, water supply, telephone services, railways), where the large capital requirements and entry costs limited competition. With such 'natural monopoly' enterprises there was a special need for state regulation to check private sector abuse.

Like import liberalization, Latin American divestiture programmes commonly went through at great speed. So privatization revenues often peaked in the early 1990s and then fell, partly because there

were few marketable assets left, partly because of political contro-
versy over the dubious methods used to sell public property and over
the inadequate regulation of divested concerns. Brazil was in some
measure an exception on these points. Here divestiture made a rather
slow start in the early 1990s and then gathered pace towards the end
of the decade, when the country took more than half Latin America's
privatization revenue (Manzetti 1999; ECLAC 2000: 52). For the
region as a whole, about 60 per cent of privatization income came
through purchases by foreign investors, who were re-admitted to
utilities, mining, and oil production, sectors from which outside
ownership had been almost completely excluded under ISI. As a
contrast, in East Asia nearly all disposals went to national firms.
However, there were wide differences between Latin American
countries. In the smaller and poorer republics, outside capital took an
80–90 per cent share; nationalist feeling against foreign encroachment played a major role in the anti-privatization backlash. In Brazil,
on the other hand, with a strong indigenous business class, the
foreign share reached only about 45 per cent. Apart from privatization opportunities, neoliberal reform encouraged DFI by creating
customs unions and by relaxing joint venture and local content rules.

Free market advocates claim that all these policy changes were
required to improve economic performance. Neoliberal theory pre-
dicts that reduced external tariffs, greater competition, and better
access to imported inputs, should stimulate major advances in manufacturing efficiency. Firms will be encouraged to specialize and build
up foreign sales in lines for which they are best suited. The balance
of payments will be strengthened, as exports soon outstrip any initial
surge of imports, and long-term output growth will improve. Neoliberals justify the sale of state enterprises by claiming that private
sector management will almost invariably be superior, at least under
Latin American conditions. DFI brings in new capital with improved
technology that can 'spill over' to nationally owned firms.

Statists, on the other hand, while now usually conceding that ISI
protectionism had been excessive, claim that tariff reduction came
too abruptly, coinciding as it often did with REER appreciations that
also lowered the cost of imported goods. At the same time divestiture programmes and cuts in general government spending denied
private sector business other, hitherto important, forms of state assistance. Thus, the argument runs, many enterprises which might have
been viable, if allowed to adapt over a longer period, were bankrupted instead (Buxton and Phillips 1999a: 21). Research and
development programmes had been almost entirely funded by the

public sector, so austerity measures weakened Latin America's tech-nological base (Green 1995: 125–6). Industry's share of Latin American GDP fell after 1990 (Table 2.2). The biggest firms, some of them national but mostly foreign-owned, could use their superior financial power to rationalize and re-equip with high-productivity imported machinery. They also looked abroad for component supplies. So the smaller firms and the more labour-intensive activities lost ground. Industry's share of the workforce fell, even though industrial output sometimes began to recover quite rapidly soon after the start of liberalization. Unemployment, and the shift of displaced labour to inferior service sector occupations, widened pay gaps between high- and low-skilled workers (Stallings and Peres 2000: 153–201; Amann and Baer 2002: 955). This aggravated income inequality and social tensions.

Mismanaged privatizations further threatened the legitimacy of the reform process. SOE divestiture was often rushed through under emergency conditions at knock-down prices, and without adequate restraint on monopoly abuses. In Latin America under liberalization most foreign investment took over or refurbished existing assets, rather than creating new capacity in export manufacturing, as was usually the case in East Asia. Much Latin American DFI came through utility privatization, and so went into the supply of 'non-tradeable' (i.e. non-exportable) products, telephone services most notably, pleasant perhaps for consumers, but doing little to curb balance of payments deficits. Profit remittances to foreign owners became a growing burden on the external account. Quite high levels of DFI could be accompanied by economic stagnation or decline (Table 3.1, column 8).

Neoliberal export drives, in South America at least, relied, above all, on natural resource-based commodities. For example, Chile's recovery during the later 1980s entailed the development of certain 'non-traditional' lines (fruit, wine, timber, fish) to supplement copper, the established staple (Collins and Lear 1994; Green 1995: 216–7). Statists argue that this approach is vulnerable to terms of trade deter-ioration from the long-term decline in commodity prices, and that output will soon be constrained by environmental degradation. The fact that the production of raw materials entails limited labour force skill further restricts their dynamic potential (Pietrobelli 1998). Only Mexico and some of the smaller Caribbean basin republics have made much progress with manufactured exports, through access to the nearby US market under regional trade agreements. However, statists suggest that prospects here are clouded by foreign ownership, enclave characteristics, and mounting competition from China's huge reserve of low-cost labour. In Mexico export assembly was concentrated in the *maquiladoras* along the northern border with the US. They relied almost entirely on imported inputs and had few links to the rest of the Mexican economy (Sklair 1989). For much of the 1990s Latin American balance of trade deficits widened, especially in high-technology manufactured goods.

Nevertheless, there are also grounds for a more optimistic view of the new economic model. In the later 1990s the Latin American foreign trade performance began to strengthen, increasing the region's share of world exports for the first time since the 1940s. Relatively strong export growth is, as a rule, associated with above-average output per head gains (Table 3.1, column 5). Commodity prices remained more resilient after the 1997–8 East Asian crisis than during the 1980s, when Latin America's terms of trade deteriorated by about 30 per cent. As a contrast there has been no further net change in the region's terms of trade over the last 15 years. The aggregate regional current account deficit reached a peak as a share of GDP in 1998 and subsequently narrowed. Improvement resulted partly through new DFI-based export projects coming on stream, and partly through devaluations to restore competitive exchange rates, in Mexico from 1995, in Brazil from 1999, and Argentina from 2002 (see below). A number of detailed studies show particular sectors, for example the Brazilian shoe industry, adjusting to market challenges with reorganization and increased productivity (Schmitz 1999). In Mexico, *maquila* export assembly spread southwards from the border zone and made greater use of local inputs (Blair and Gereffi 2001).

For Latin America as a whole the decline in industry's share of GDP was a one-off result of trade liberalization, which eliminated some capacity, and caused the relative price of manufactured goods to fall. Since the early 1990s industry's output share has been rising again (Reinhardt and Peres 2000: 1549). Furthermore, the job losses and unemployment growth caused by restructuring were limited by the extent to which Latin American ISI had relied on labour-saving, capital-intensive techniques. There was no overall growth of income differentials in the 1990s following import liberalization. It seems that reduced business profits and cheaper manufactured goods for the population at large offset the inequality-widening effects from the displacement of industrial workers. The main inequality growth had occurred earlier, during the 1980s, the consequence of the debt crisis and high inflation (Thorp 1998: 352–3;

Stallings and Peres 2000: 129–42; Vanden and Prevost 2002: 102–3; World Bank 2003: 236–7).

Most of the larger Latin American private sector firms withstood the increased penetration by foreign capital. Certain indigenous companies, for example the Mexican cement manufacturer Cemex, and the Brazilian steel producer Gerdau, expanded by acquisitions abroad. As time passed, introducing better regulation and more competitive business regimes went some way to correct the defects of hasty privatization. In Latin America's post-1990 fast growers, the public sector share of investment has been comparatively modest, a definite contrast with the slow growers, except for Argentina. The total investment rate, on the other hand, does not differ between the two groups (Table 3.1, columns 9 and 10). Thus, it seems that an enlarged private sector role has benefited efficiency. Neo-structuralists concede that SOE divestiture has improved standards of utility management (Stallings and Peres 2000: 186–91). Greater efficiency in non-tradeable infrastructure services, for example rail freight, can strengthen export competitiveness and the balance of payments.

Nevertheless, the neoliberal reforms quite clearly still have severe limitations. Privatized SOEs had accounted for only about 5 per cent of regional GDP, and employed only about 2–3 per cent of the labour force, so the potential impact from productivity gains here was modest. The post-1998 narrowing of current account deficits entailed slower output growth to limit domestic demand. In most countries inequality may not have risen over recent years, but it has persisted at a relatively high level. Neoliberal predictions that earnings differentials would narrow through a shift to labour-intensive, export-led development of the East Asian type remain unfulfilled. Latin American averages, dominated by Brazil and Mexico, cover highly unfavourable trends in employment and income distribution for some other republics. Thus, while across the region as a whole between the mid-1980s and the mid-1990s industry's share of the labour force declined slightly, from about 24 per cent to about 23 per cent, for Argentina, where ISI self-sufficiency had been carried to extremes and where liberalization was especially abrupt, the corresponding figures are 33 per cent and 25 per cent (World Bank 2001b). Argentina's urban unemployment rate reached 17.5 per cent in the mid-1990s, twice the regional average (Stallings and Peres 2000: 120).

So, might better results have come through more gradual reform, with a less complete dismantling of industrial policy, as statists claim? This seems doubtful. First, delaying tariff cuts and SOE divestiture would have held back or even prevented macroeconomic stabilization. Second, the record suggests that most Latin American countries lack the political conditions for taking a selective, discriminating approach to industrial support at a reasonable cost, insulated from vested interests. During the 1960s and 1970s lobbying by firms established under ISI had compromised several attempts at piece-meal trade liberalization (Morawetz 1981: 98–9; Frieden 1991: 196). Chile is sometimes seen as a possible exception. Standards of public administration here are unusually high, so perhaps government should have done more to promote industrial upgrading that built on free market success with natural resource exports (Green 1995: 134; Pietrobelli 1998). However, Chilean manufacturing was making a strong recovery in the last years of the 1973–89 military dictatorship, with little direct public sector assistance, but then lost momentum in the 1990s after a civilian government sympathetic to neo-structuralist intervention had taken charge.

Financial liberalization and international capital flows

Financial liberalization dismantled the statist devices which had been used to promote ISI by influencing the allocation of credit, for example interest rate ceilings, low-cost loans for favoured borrowers, and the requirement that banks place a large part of their reserves in government hands. Public sector banks, many of them recently nationalized (the case with Chile and Mexico) were transferred to private ownership. The lifting of exchange controls permitted the free movement of funds between national and foreign currencies. Neoliberal doctrine held that these reforms would encourage savings, by offering improved returns, and help ensure that capital was used more efficiently (Edwards 1995: 200–51).

However, in practice, rapid liberalization often caused severe financial volatility and banking crises. The first such episode affected Chile and the other Southern Cone republics in the late 1970s and early 1980s. The higher interest rates permitted here under the new financial regime, and used to curb inflation, soon attracted large inflows of foreign money. Much of these funds were channelled through the deregulated banking systems as credit for buying foreign cars, cameras, watches, and other luxury imported goods, to which consumers had been given access by tariff liberalization. At the same time, the capital inflows raised REERs and made exporting more difficult. Large trade deficits resulted. Lending booms of this type were unsustainable, because they did not finance productive investment. But according to the raw neoliberalism that influenced Southern Cone policy at this stage, private sector debtors and creditors should be 'rational', capable of judging transactions for themselves, without detailed official oversight. Nevertheless, as the situation became more precarious, governments intervened. They borrowed abroad to support national currencies at increasingly over-valued rates, with the aim of controlling inflation and preventing a banking collapse, while private wealth holders, fearing an imminent devaluation, converted assets into foreign currency and transferred them abroad. In the Southern Cone, accelerating flight capital out-flows were a main cause of the early 1980s debt crisis. Large-scale capital flight also occurred at the same time from Mexico, where the long border with the US made financial controls difficult to enforce, and from Venezuela, relatively 'open' because of its oil industry. By 1983 about US$160 billion of privately owned Latin American flight capital was held abroad, mainly in First World bank accounts (Banuri 1991: 18, 47–9, 75, 88–9; Frieden 1991: 158–73, 212–15; Bulmer-Thomas 1994: 338–41).

Latin America again experienced volatile international money movements in the early 1990s, when a large financial inflow, much of it repatriated flight capital, resumed for the first time since 1982. Investors were encouraged by the apparent success of the Brady debt relief plan, falling US interest rates, and the feeling that neoliberal reforms were beginning to solve Latin America's economic prob-lems. The main vehicle for investment was not bank lending, as in the 1970s, but 'portfolio' finance, the sale of Latin American bonds and shares, often in newly privatized businesses. The recession which affected the developed countries in the early 1990s helped to stimu-late enthusiasm for the high returns offered by 'emerging' stockmarkets. Between 1991 and 1993 Mexico was the leading Third World recipient of foreign capital, attracting US$75 billion. The influx raised the REER and held back exports. Then, in January 1994, US interest rates began to rise once more. At the same time a rural uprising broke out unexpectedly in the southern Mexican state of Chiapas, evoking memories of the country's violent past. (The Chiapas rebels called themselves Zapatistas, after a peasant leader of the 1910–20 revolution.) A few weeks later investors were further alarmed by the assassination of the governing party's presidential election candidate, and they began selling off Mexican securities on a massive scale. The central bank's foreign currency reserves fell by $25 billion in the course of the year, forcing a devaluation and austerity measures that once more put the country into deep recession (Green 1995: 85–7). The Mexican crisis also shook other Latin American countries, especially Argentina, where in 1991 the currency had been made fully convertible, to limit inflation, attract money from abroad, and underwrite an ambitious privatization programme. Costly government bail-outs of insolvent banks put a severe strain on public sector finances.

Statists emphasize the damage done by these episodes of instability, noticing how the 1994–5 'tequila' crisis had a comparatively slight effect in Colombia and Chile, which both maintained quite stringent financial controls, reintroduced by Chile after 1982 (Ffrench-Davis 2000: 101–28, 195–216). Some neoliberals admit that serious mistakes were made in the early stages of financial reform, by proceeding too rapidly before an adequate macroeconomic equilibrium had been established (Edwards 1995: 295–317). Certainly, there is no evidence that permitting higher interest rates has encouraged savings. Latin American private sector savings fell in the early 1990s, offsetting the reduction of government budget deficits, because trade liberalization cut business profits and encouraged consumption booms. Fiscal deficits then often widened again later in the decade, reducing the aggregate savings level. The persistent weakness of Latin American savings, even in many fast-growth republics, is a notable contrast with East Asia (Table 3.1, columns 11–13).

On the positive side, since the mid-1990s international movements of 'hot' short-term money have been less important as a source of disruption in Latin America. The change results partly from closer official oversight but, above all, from investors learning through experience of the risks involved. Portfolio equity inflows to Latin American stockmarkets have not yet regained the 1993–4 speculative peak. Instead, DFI, longer term and less erratic, has become much the largest category of external finance. This included many foreign takeovers of Latin American banks, ensuring more careful loan management. By 2000 half the banking assets in Mexico, Argentina, and Chile were foreign owned.

The most recent crises originate, above all, from domestic problems, with sudden international money flows the symptom rather than the cause of stress. Thus, in 1999, accelerating capital flight forced Brazil to abandon its crawling peg exchange rate mechanism and allow a more rapid devaluation. Confidence had been undermined by the country's large fiscal deficits. A reluctance to put up interest rates the previous year, as the Brazilian president sought re-election, coinciding with financial turmoil in East Asia and Russia, brought matters to a head. Brazil's devaluation stimulated exports. Some progress was made on curbing budget imbalances. Privatization sales still attracted DFI. Creditors, domestic and foreign, were reassured, and economic growth could continue at a modest pace.

However, there were painful consequences in Argentina, where the *Mercosur* customs union had made exporters heavily reliant on sales to Brazil. The loss of competitiveness against Brazilian products, and depressed world markets for farm commodities, sent Argentina into recession. There was an alarming increase in the share of export earnings taken by foreign debt interest payments (Table 2.5). The fiscal deficit widened. Unlike Brazil, Argentina had few state enterprises left that might generate privatization revenue. Furthermore, Argentina's inflexible currency law prevented the country from following the Brazilian example of devaluation. So, instead, the government tried to balance its books with tax increases and spending cuts, aggravating the recession. Unemployment, already high, rose further. Splits opened up within the ruling coalition, an uncomfortable alliance between centre-right and leftist parties. During 2001 attempts to defend the exchange rate through austerity measures became more desperate. First World money markets expressed their scepticism by demanding higher interest rates on new loans. Capital flight gathered pace, forcing the government, in December 2001, to impose a freeze on bank deposits. Rioting crowds from the devastated industrial suburbs of Buenos Aires then made common cause with middle-class street protestors, enraged at the deposit freeze, and forced the government to give up office. An interim president abandoned the exchange rate peg and declared a debt moratorium, at $132 billion the world's largest ever default, leaving the national finances in acute disarray. GDP fell by about 10 per cent.

Argentina's spectacular crisis occurred under local circumstances that were distinctive in many respects. Neoliberal reform here had been unusually rapid and far-reaching, the reaction to a particularly acute case of ISI exhaustion. No other major Latin American country had attempted to maintain a fixed exchange rate over such a long period. Nowhere else did liberalization entail such severe industrial job losses and long-term unemployment. On the other hand, as we shall see (Chapter 5), Latin America currently has many similar examples of political conflict and precarious coalition government, which may yet bring similar economic misfortune.

Conclusion

Neoliberal reform has had useful economic effects in Latin America, statist criticisms notwithstanding, even though it is now obvious, with hindsight, that on some points adjustment might have been better managed. Many privatizations were poorly regulated. Financial liberalization was often premature. However, on the whole rapid reform matched Latin America's needs. A legacy of high inflation and fiscal deficits from the ISI period made the more gradualist approach taken elsewhere quite unsuitable for the region. This background, and chronically low savings, are the main reasons why Latin America has not matched East Asian growth rates, and shows little prospect of doing so. Thus far, at least, the benefits of macroeconomic stabilization have outweighed the political costs of restructuring, but Argentina has been noticed as a possible exception and there are other cases still to consider, Venezuela in particular.

How seriously has the international context disadvantaged Latin America in the liberalization period? Levels of foreign indebtedness seem to have had a significant, though not overwhelming, influence on recent economic performance. After deteriorating sharply during the debt crisis years, the region's terms of trade showed little further change from the late 1980s. But other damaging external forces may also have been at work. For example, to what extent do Colombia's deteriorating fortunes result from the poisonous effects of international drug trafficking, or Cuba's from the embargo maintained against the island by the US? These issues are pursued in Chapters 4 and 5.

4   Latin America and the wider world

Chapter 1 noticed how the East Asian NICs' economic success has called into question dependency theory, and its argument that Latin American problems result largely from the effects of First World capitalism. Nevertheless, while the dependency perspective may not be equally valid for all developing regions, does it still offer useful insights on Latin America? Have international circumstances here been particularly unfavourable, perhaps more so than in East Asia?

Latin America is part of the Western Hemisphere, lying at a distance from Europe, Africa, and Asia, but close to the US, for most of the twentieth century the world's richest and most powerful country. Possible advantages of this location include ready access to the US as an export market and as a source of investment. Latin America escaped the destructive effects of the two world wars. Spending by North American tourists, and the earnings of emigrant workers in the US, have made important contributions to the national income of Mexico and other Caribbean basin countries. However, US pre-eminence may also have been unhelpful to Latin America in various ways. This chapter considers whether the US has had seriously damaging effects on its southern neighbours, through political intervention, through trade policy, through the financial leverage associated with the debt crisis, and through the stimulus given by North American demand to the Latin American narcotics industry. It is argued here that since 1945 Latin America as a whole has not, in fact, been handicapped to any great extent by unfavourable external circumstances. The harm caused by the US in the region is often exaggerated.

US intervention

US claims to a special leadership role in the Western Hemisphere began with the declaration by President Monroe in 1823, following

Latin American independence, that the Americas should not be subject to any new colonization from outside the region. The enormous growth of US economic strength during the later nineteenth century made the country more aggressive. The Monroe doctrine was extended under Theodore Roosevelt's presidency (1901–8) to justify armed 'police' intervention in neighbouring states, when their chronic disorder and failure to pay foreign creditors might provoke interference by European powers. However, by the 1920s, account had to be taken of growing Latin American nationalist feeling, itself partly a response to overbearing US behaviour. In the 1930s, economic depression checked US assertiveness, and President Franklin Roosevelt's 'good neighbor' policy repudiated interventionism. Then the Second World War revived the US economy, restored national self-confidence, and made the country determined to take a leading international role. By 1945 the US accounted for more than half the world's industrial production, completely eclipsing former European rivals in Latin American investment and trade (Keen and Haynes 2000: 542–56).

From the later 1940s the main US foreign policy concern became the threat of communist expansion posed by the Soviet Union and China. Western Europe and East Asia, the front lines in the cold war, were to be held by direct US military engagement, combined with generous support for economic reconstruction. (US aid amounted to 5–10 per cent of national income in Taiwan and South Korea during the 1950s.) The Western Hemisphere was less immediately at risk and could be secured more cheaply, through a system of US-led treaties. The US urged its Latin American allies to sever diplomatic ties with the Soviet Union and outlaw local communist parties. Washington feared that communist-inspired labour unrest within the region threatened the supply of strategic raw materials. Very little economic aid was forthcoming, but the US supplied instruction and equipment to Latin American militaries. The onset of the cold war apparently checked the progressive political tendencies that had affected Latin America in the mid-1940s, inspired by the US–Soviet alliance against Nazi Germany. From 1948 a number of recently established reforming governments were overthrown by the armed forces, with US approval or acquiescence (Bethell and Roxborough 1992). The swing to the right in US domestic politics induced by the cold war led to the election of the Republican Dwight Eisenhower as president. Several important posts in his administration (1953–60) were held by men drawn from business. Their hostility to Latin

America's government-backed ISI provided a further reason for with-holding economic assistance (Skidmore and Smith 2001: 368–76).

The US modified its policy when the 1959 Cuban Revolution showed that a corrupt, immobile dictatorship gave inadequate protection against communism. President Kennedy's Alliance for Progress offered finance for economic development and social reform, but this was combined with programmes to strengthen Latin American counter-insurgency capabilities. 'National security doctrine', emphasizing the armed forces' role as guardians against international communism, gave ideological support to a new wave of military coups, most notably in Brazil (1964) and Argentina (1962, 1966). Later, the US worked actively to destabilize the Marxist-influenced government of Salvador Allende in Chile. Therefore, it is argued, US cold war anxieties may have reinforced Latin American authoritarianism, thwarted efforts to put development on a more secure, equitable basis, and aggravated political instability (Sheahan 1987: 340–54; Smith 1994; Smith 1996; Keen and Haynes 2000: 556–77).

> The worst side of external pressure is not the operation of the world economy in general but the quite specific intervention of the US. At the same time as the US provides real help in many contexts it has constituted a persistent force on the side of repression whenever any signs of communist influence can be detected
> (Sheahan 1987: 361).

Nevertheless, the significance of the US in Latin American politics should not be exaggerated. First, we must distinguish between the small Caribbean basin republics, which have been highly susceptible to external pressure, and the rest of Latin America (including Mexico), which has enjoyed much greater autonomy. In the Caribbean and Central America, the US has often prevailed simply by bringing overwhelming strength to bear against limited opposition, as with the seizure of the territory required for building the Panama Canal (1903). US troops administered Nicaragua (1912–33), Haiti (1915–34), the Dominican Republic (1916–24), and Cuba (1917–23). Subsequently, US-trained National Guards sustained notorious client dictators: the Somozas in Nicaragua, and Rafael Trujillo in the Dominican Republic (Rouquié 1987: 120–8). The US backed the invasion that brought down Guatemala's reformist government in 1954 (Gleijeses 1991). US forces have been deployed more recently in Grenada (1983) and Panama (1989).

However, such direct action was not feasible elsewhere. Any political interference attempted in the larger republics had to be undertaken through local proxies. Some authors emphasize the closeties cultivated by the US with Latin America's armed forces, through military aid, and through training programmes that inculcated a cold war, anti-communist mentality (Keen and Haynes 2000: 597). The difficulty here is that fear of communism was already firmly established by the 1930s in Latin American upper-class and military circles, without any encouragement from the US. So arguably the 1944–6 'social democratic opening' should be seen as anomalous, an expression of the euphoria generated by the wartime US–Soviet alliance, while the subsequent reaction was a return to 'routine politics' (Bethell 1994b: 137, 175–80, 328–9). In any case, despite the 'conservative consolidation' of the early cold war period, during the 1950s elected civilian regimes were the most common Latin American government type, and populist leaders had a substantial influence. The more widespread shift in the 1960s to military dictatorship was provoked mainly by domestic influences, though the US and its cold war concerns may have played a secondary, conditioning role (Chapter 5; Rouquié 1987: 117–50).

Apart from the possibilities for military intervention, the US has also had a powerful economic hold over its smaller neighbours. Until the 1959 revolution Cuba was kept in a state of abject and demoralized subordination by the island's reliance on the US as a market for its sugar. Some of the Central American republics depended heavily on the US-controlled banana trade. But, once again, the position else-where was quite different. Strong nationalist feelings had developed and they were still asserted even if government became more socially conservative. For example, Chile's swing to the right after 1947 was accompanied by further increases in the tax rates placed on US copper mining companies, an imposition which Washington felt obliged to accept (Moran 1974: 24, 176–9).

It is not clear that US economic assistance gave South Korea and Taiwan a significant advantage over Latin America. Both countries had suffered extensive war damage, and both were obliged to maintain large armed forces against threatening communist neighbours. Some authors imply that the US exercised leverage as an aid donor to ensure that South Korea and Taiwan implemented land reforms, and other helpful measures (Haggard 1990: 67–70; Green 1995: 181–2). However, the two countries ignored US advice on other points, for example by maintaining interventionist industrial policies. When substantial US aid did reach Latin America, for Bolivia after its 1952 revolution (Keen and Haynes 2000: 559), and the region as a whole after 1960, very little was achieved.

Finally, from the mid-1960s various international developments weakened the US position in Latin America. Washington was distracted by the Vietnam War, by the Middle East, and by the pursuit of improved relations with the Soviet Union and China. Cold war tensions eased. The Soviet Union and Cuba worked hard to conciliate Latin American opinion by distancing themselves from strategies of armed revolution. Moscow established or re-established a diplomatic representation in most of the region's capitals. The economic resurgence of Western Europe and Japan provided a commercial counterweight to the US in the Americas.

This changing context gave Latin American governments extra room for manoeuvre. Some of the military rulers who gained power in the later 1960s did not view communism as a serious threat, took a radical 'anti-imperialist' line, and launched ambitious schemes for social reform. Panama's General Torrijos pursued the issue of US sovereignty over the Canal Zone. In Peru, General Velasco's administration (1968–75) expropriated most of the large landed estates. It also nationalized several important US enterprises, without offering satisfactory compensation. Washington withheld official aid and credits, but Peru defeated the financial blockade by securing Euro-currency loans from commercial banks. Foreign capital was secured for an ambitious new copper mining project on the strength of sales prospects in Europe and Japan. Armaments were supplied by the Soviet Union. The severe difficulties eventually encountered by Peru's reformist experiment resulted more from national mismanagement than external pressures (Rouquié 1987: 312–18; Sheahan 1987: 257–65; Stallings 1987: 271–9).

The US showed intense hostility to Salvador Allende's government in Chile, because of his Marxist orientation. However, despite allegations made at the time, it is doubtful whether the US Central Intelligence Agency's schemes for economic sabotage and political destabilization made a decisive contribution to Allende's overthrow by the military in 1973 (Martz 1988: 167–8). The other authoritarian coups of the period, in Uruguay (1973) and Argentina (1976), certainly occurred without significant US involvement.

Critical accounts of the US impact on Latin American politics often stress the influence of the large US-owned multinational corporate enterprises which have been so prominent in the region. It is claimed that countries seeking foreign investment had to offer the reassurance of a 'safe' business climate, with a docile, low-cost labour force, secured by political repression. The regional trend towards military dictatorship after 1960 has been explained partly in these terms. During the early stages of ISI, the argument runs, Latin American manufacturing was mainly controlled by indigenous entrepreneurs and dedicated to supplying a mass market with relatively simple products (for example clothing, shoes, furniture). Businessmen, therefore, benefited from high wages to ensure a widely distributed purchasing power, and favoured democratic, populist regimes. However, the MNCs' entry shifted industry towards luxury durables, and required a greater income concentration in the hands of the rich to ensure a sufficient demand (Evans 1979: 29–38; Keen and Haynes 2000: 586).

The lobbying power of large firms in Washington perhaps encouraged US action to prevent Latin American reform. The United Fruit Company's connections with the Eisenhower administration allegedly provoked the 1954 intervention against Guatemala, where the company's banana plantations were under threat. ITT, a US conglomerate, reacted to the expropriation of its Chilean business in the early 1970s by urging action against the Allende government (Keen and Haynes 2000: 559–63). 'Latin American democracy could have been healthier in the last generation if foreign investment had been ruled out' (Sheahan 1987: 360).

All these points seem questionable. The main causes of income inequality are to be found in nationally determined patterns of landownership, industrial structure, and social welfare provision (Chapters 5 and 6). The MNCs cannot be held primarily responsible for the US government's anti-reformist interventions in Latin America. Several studies show that since 1945 strategic security objectives have taken precedence over business interests in determining US foreign policy. For example, it now seems that, contrary to allegations made at the time, the US action against Guatemala in 1954 was provoked by well-founded reports of communist infiltration, and not by the United Fruit Company's lobbying (Gleijeses 1991: 361–6). Indeed, many US firms doing business in Latin America were reluctant to seek help from Washington, judging that this would increase nationalist hostility. A provocative stance of the type taken by ITT against the Allende government in Chile came to be seen as outdated and unhelpful (Martz 1988: 45–52; Lowenthal 1991: 142–73).

During his term of office (1977–80) President Carter tried to give a new high-principled, moral tone to US foreign relations. Military equipment and economic aid were withheld from Latin American governments which had unsatisfactory records on human rights. Carter negotiated the eventual handover of the Canal Zone to Panama. He ensured a democratic transfer of power in the Dominican Republic. He may have deterred an army coup in Bolivia. The withdrawal of US support from Somoza assisted the Sandinista victory in Nicaragua. But Carter's approach achieved little in the larger republics. Brazil and Argentina responded to his embargo on military supplies by purchasing weaponry elsewhere, and by promoting their own armaments industries. When denied US nuclear technology they turned to Germany instead. The Soviet Union provided shipments of uranium. In 1960, 75 per cent of Latin America's arms imports came from the US. That figure had fallen to 20 per cent by 1970 and 7 per cent by 1980 (Smith 1994: 11).

The Reagan administration began in 1981 by rededicating national policy to a world-wide struggle against Soviet communism, and showed a renewed warmth towards Latin America's dictatorships as useful allies. However, once again the course of Latin American events failed to match US preferences, and a strong regional movement away from authoritarian rule soon began, accelerated by the downfall of the Argentine miltary junta after the defeat of its attempt to occupy the Falkland Islands in 1982, an adventure undertaken against strong US advice. The debt crisis then reinforced the trend, which Washington felt obliged to accept with good grace. So, the promotion of democracy became a major rhetorical theme of Ronald Reagan's presidency, partly as justification for his obsessive campaign against Nicaragua's Sandinista government (Carothers 1991), and the stance has been maintained by subsequent occupants of the White House. The Soviet Union's chronic internal weaknesses became increasingly obvious, leading to its loss of control over Eastern Europe and final breakup in 1989–91. The end of the Cold War made it unnecessary for the US to continue backing authoritarian regimes, a fact that, during the later 1980s, helped oust all of Latin America's few remaining dictators, except for Fidel Castro on Cuba. Since then, US influence has been applied against actual or threatened military coups in Venezuela (1992), Guatemala (1993), Paraguay (1996, 1999), and Ecuador (2000), ensuring that at least an appearance of democratic civilian rule continued. However, Washington tolerated the use of the army to strengthen executive power by Peru's President Fujimori, seen as a useful ally in combating the narcotics trade (see below), and was slow to condemn an abortive coup that briefly deposed Hugo Chávez, Venezuela's radical populist president (2002).

US trade policy

Over nearly four decades after the Second World War, US foreign trade policy concentrated on promoting international commerce by multilateral negotiation through the General Agreement on Tariffs and Trade (GATT). Washington shunned bilateral (country to country) and preferential trading bloc arrangements, believing that in the past they had been one of European imperialism's most pernicious features and a cause of international conflict. GATT diplomacy cut back the First World countries' industrial tariff protection, stimulated trade between them in manufactures, and created opportunities for Third World export-led industrialization, taken by the NICs. Latin America got few benefits, because of its commitment to ISI, and because the GATT process neglected agriculture. However, except for post-1959 Cuba (see below) the region never suffered systematic US discrimination in trade policy. Washington did not retaliate in kind against Latin American protectionism, or try to keep the dominant position secured by US exporters when competition from Europe and Japan was eliminated during the Second World War. The US share of Latin American imports fell from about 60 per cent in 1945 to 35 per cent by 1980. The proportion of US exports taken by Latin America fell from about a third to 17 per cent over the same period (Smith 1996: 342). On one point the US acted against its own immediate economic interests by backing the creation, in the 1960s, of the International Coffee Organization (ICO), a market support scheme, even though US consumers absorbed half the world's coffee exports, mainly from Latin American sources. Following the 1959 Cuban Revolution, Washington was afraid that falling coffee prices threatened the political stability of Brazil and Colombia, the two main producers (Bates 1997: 121–6).

Since the early 1980s, US trade multilateralism has been qualified by a new interest in regional agreements. The initial policy shift reflected growing doubts over the country's economic competitiveness, and impatience at the slowdown of GATT negotiations. So, the North American Free Trade Agreement (NAFTA), embracing the US, Canada, and Mexico, was concluded in 1993. For the US, one of NAFTA's main purposes was to check the upsurge of illegal immigration from Mexico that followed the early 1980s debt crisis, by stimulating more employment growth 'south of the border'. Washington also promoted the Free-Trade Area of the Americas (FTAA), to cover all the Western Hemisphere, except Cuba. NAFTA has greatly strengthened US–Mexican economic ties, probably with beneficial results for Mexico (Chapter 3), but the FTAA scheme is moving slowly and seems unlikely to be completed by 2005, the target date. The obstacles to progress include concerns within the US over 'cheap labour' import competition. Powerful US domestic farming interests, heavily subsidized and protected, feel under threat because the FTAA involves countries, for example Brazil and Argentina, which are major agricultural exporters, unlike Mexico. The immigration issue is a less compelling reason for trade liberalization with South American countries, at a greater distance from the US. Furthermore, the ICO and world coffee prices collapsed in 1989, it is suggested because the triumph of neoliberal ideology and the relaxation of cold war concerns made Washington repudiate market intervention (Bates 1997: 173–5). So, aspects of recent US trade policy may have been unhelpful to Latin America.

Yet, various qualifying points must be made. The ICO's demise was only a secondary cause of the coffee price decline, which came, above all, from new planting and expanded output in response to market scarcity in the late 1970s. Since 1999, prices have been depressed further through the exports generated by Vietnam's economic liberalization, and by new high-yield cultivation techniques in Brazil. On the issue of tariff policy, the Caribbean Basin Initiative (1983), while not covering sugar, confirmed or slightly extended the preferential access of other exports from Central America to the US. (The scheme was aimed at counteracting subversion from communist Cuba and Sandinista Nicaragua, and excluded these two countries.) In 1990, similar preferences were granted to Colombia and the other northern Andean republics as part of the 'war on drugs' (see below). More generally, Latin America could benefit from the relative dynamism of the US economy since the early 1980s neoliberal Reagan initiatives. Over the last two decades the US has been the major force in world trade expansion. Thus, during the 1990s, the country's imports from all sources grew by 105 per cent and from Latin America by 280 per cent (340 per cent from Mexico, 200 per cent from elsewhere in the region), although the voracious US appetite for imported goods may not be sustainable (Chapter 9). As a contrast, in Western Europe neoliberal reform made little progress, except for Great Britain under Mrs Thatcher, and the region has never fully recovered from the 1970s growth slowdown. The European Union with its grotesque Common Agricultural Policy, considerably more protectionist and distorting than the US farm subsidy regime, increased imports from Latin America by only 50 per cent during the 1990s (World Bank 2001b: 216, 325).

However, the US treatment of Cuba seems more clearly vindictive and malign. Washington responded to Fidel Castro's 1959 Revolution by imposing a comprehensive economic embargo, followed at first by every other country in the Western Hemisphere except Canada and Mexico. Cuba became dependent on the Soviet Union, exchanging sugar for Russian oil on special terms, and suffering acute economic distress when the collapse of the Soviet regime in the early 1990s ended this arrangement. The US dealt with surviving communist dictatorships in China and Vietnam through 'constructive engagement', but still tried to isolate Cuba. The Torricelli Act (1992) made complete regime change and democratization on the island prerequisites for lifting the embargo. The Helms-Burton Act (1996) tightened sanctions further. These measures reflected US anger that communism had gained a foothold in America's 'backyard', belief that a small, weak neighbour could be bullied into complete submission, and the political leverage of virulently anti-Castro Cuban exiles concentrated in Florida, an election swing state (Morley and McGillion 2002).

US conduct has certainly damaged Cuba, but is not wholly responsible for the island's difficulties. Some external influences should be working in Cuba's favour. Europe, Canada, and most Latin American countries, have tried to demonstrate their independence from Washington since the end of the cold war by cultivating ties with the Castro regime. The US has not fully enforced its own embargoes. Substantial emigrant remittances are reaching Cuba, about $1 billion a year (4 per cent of GDP) by 2002. On the domestic side, Castro's personal dictatorship limits economic reform, entailing gross inefficiencies through the continued commitment to socialism, and holds back the improvement of relations with the outside world (Appendix 1, Biographies; Wiarda and Kline 2000: 430–4).

Foreign debt and international finance

In recent years, Latin America's relations with the wider world have been dominated by the issue of debt. Following its rapid growth during the 1970s, international bank lending to the region fell sharply after 1982. Inflows of new money were exceeded by outflows of interest payments. Between 1983 and 1990, the annual resource transfer from Latin America to foreign creditors averaged about 3 per cent of regional output, a severe drain (Bethell 1994a: 245). From 1991, a net capital inflow resumed, but foreign debt interest payments still took about 2 per cent of regional GDP.

Quite clearly, indebtedness has become one of Latin America's most serious problems. Chapter 2 presented it as a symptom or consequence of more fundamental internal weaknesses during the ISI period, rather than as an external imposition. Because Latin American export earnings did not meet import requirements, foreign borrowing had to cover current account balance of payments deficits. However, Latin America may also have been put at a disadvantage by the workings of international money markets.

During the 1970s, First World banks competed with each other to attract the funds accumulated by the Middle East oil producers following the OPEC price increases. Profitable uses then had to be found for the petrodollar deposits, and with the developed countries in recession, Latin America seemed one of the most promising outlets. Its governments were pursuing plausible development plans. Natural resource abundance gave the region good prospects as source of raw materials exports, and it was widely assumed at the time that commodity prices would rise over the long term. International banks were already well established in Latin America, and they hoped to enlarge their presence. So, it is suggested, First World bankers actively 'pushed' loans onto Latin American borrowers. The fall in interest rates charged, and various other indicators, give some support to the thesis that the growth of lending was driven by supply-side influences (Stallings 1987: 161–85; Frieden 1991: 53–66; Green 1991: 73–4). Then, in the early 1980s, Latin America suffered the double blow of a sudden rise in interest rates, when the US and British governments adopted monetarist economic policies, combined with depressed export demand for raw materials. Mexico's difficulties were most acute, because it was so reliant on oil sales and vulnerable to capital flight, undermining lenders' confidence in Latin America as a whole through a 'contagion effect' (Banuri 1991: 22). The debt crisis may, therefore, be said to have resulted largely from the operation of external forces.

However, these arguments are open to a number of objections. Some resource-abundant Asian countries, for example Malaysia and Indonesia, benefited from the 1970s commodities boom while showing restraint as borrowers. Within Latin America there is the case of Colombia, where a distinctive pattern of domestic politics (Chapter 5) ensured financial prudence, and the foreign debt remained quite modest. The most authoritative analysis of the subject concludes that over the region as a whole, foreign banks' desire to extend credit was fully matched by Latin Americans' wish to borrow. The debt build-up resulted from the interplay of supply and demand forces. 'Despite some revisionist claims lenders were rarely "forcing" money on reluctant borrowers' (Stallings 1987: 6–7).

After the onset of the debt crisis, Latin American policy contrasted with the course followed half a century earlier, when the 1929 Wall Street crash led to a similar breakdown of international lending. In the 1930s, most Latin American countries soon defaulted (stopped payment) on their foreign debt. They became less dependent on exports, and achieved quite rapid economic recovery through inward-looking development (Bulmer-Thomas 1994: 194–237). In the 1980s, Latin America tried to honour its debts, began accepting its creditors' advice by turning away from ISI, and suffered a long recession. So why did Latin America not default once again?

The 1980s policy response was different for two reasons: first, by this time national experience had discredited ISI strategies, and second, international circumstances had changed. In the 1930s, Latin American foreign debt was held by many thousands of private US and European bondholders. They lacked political influence and their governments, still strongly influenced by laissez-faire ideology, did little to discourage Latin American default. However, in the 1980s, most Latin American debt was held by a few major developed-country banks, which had become dangerously committed or 'exposed' on their Third World lending. It was feared that defaults might make some of these banks fail, leading to a more widespread economic collapse.

Therefore, the US government coordinated agreements for the rescheduling (partial postponement) of debt payments, through negotiations involving creditor banks, the IMF, and other Washington-based agencies (Stallings 1987: 103–5; Thorp 1998: 217). Debtor countries, dealt with individually on a case-by-case basis, undertook to continue meeting their obligations, thus ensuring the creditor banks' continued solvency. Debtors were induced to accept rescheduling because it offered the prospect of further loans as a reward for 'good behaviour', though in fact additional finance did not materialize on any large scale for several years. But a coercive element was also involved through the creditors' common front, organized under US leadership. The US anti-trust legislation intended to deter collusion between firms was not applied against banks involved with the problem of Third World debt. So default by a Latin American country might be punished with complete exclusion from international money markets, even for the short-term trade credits used to finance current import/export business (Bulmer-Thomas 1994: 370). Other possible sanctions included the confiscation of assets held abroad as flight capital.

Yet, while the creditors' cartel exercised powerful leverage over debtor countries, there were some mitigating features. Washington opinion recognized that a prolonged Latin American economic down-turn might have dangerous ramifications, perhaps causing political upheavals in Mexico and further south, which would enlarge the flow of illegal migrants to the US. There was also concern for Mexico's stability as a source of oil. Thus, the feeling prevailed that creditors should not press their negotiating advantage too hard, and debtor countries should be allowed to earn the export revenue which they needed to satisfy the terms of rescheduling agreements. The Reagan administration successfully resisted congressional demands that the access of foreign goods to the US market be restricted (Martz 1988: 126), even though domestic protectionist pressures had become very strong, because of the competitive weakness shown by several national industries. The commitment of key policy makers to main-taining relatively free trade derived from neoliberal economic theory, and from their reading of economic history. The 1930s depression, it was believed, had been made worse by the general resort to 'beggar my neighbour' protective tariffs. So, during the 1980s, the US ran large trade deficits, provided a buoyant market for imports, and ensured the continued growth of world trade.

South Korea benefited from these favourable circumstances to increase its exports and maintain rapid economic growth, despite suffering a large net resource outflow through service charges on outstanding loans. However, Latin America as a whole failed to respond in the same way, because of national weaknesses in eco-nomic structure and management. Chile is an exception on this point. In 1982, the country had one of the region's heaviest debt burdens, yet, in 1984, the country began an export-led recovery that has been sustained ever since, backed by unusually effective policy implementation (Chapter 5; Hojman 1993).

As it became clear that most debtor countries were not solving their problems through a strengthened export performance, Washington began to shift away from its original strategy centred around resched-uling agreements. In 1985, US Treasury Secretary James Baker made proposals for a large increase of new international lending. The 'Baker plan' was abortive, because developed country banks witheld support, but a subsequent initiative by Treasury Secretary Nicholas Brady proved more effective. The 1989 'Brady plan' offered indebted countries the partial forgiveness or writing down of their liabilities, in return for commitments to policy reform along neoliberal lines.

The new approach was possible because since 1982 the major international banks' financial position had been improved through the accumulation of profits and the issue of new shares. Having established a stronger capital base, the banks could write off some of their Third World debt without becoming insolvent. First World governments allowed loan-loss provisions to be set against tax liabilities, in effect subsidizing debt relief (Bulmer-Thomas 1994: 373–7). Also, during the 1980s in the developed countries, especially the US, there was a considerable growth of 'securitized lending', which helped banks convert their debt claims into bonds for purchase by other investors, often at a large discount.

The Brady plan laid the basis for the resumption of large-scale capital flows to Latin America in the early 1990s, and from this point discussion of the region's engagement with international finance takes a new turn. Funds now arrived mainly on a 'portfolio' basis, through the sale of Latin American bonds and shares, rather than through the foreign bank credit which predominated in the 1970s and early 1980s. Most bank lending had come from a few major firms, whose business scale gave them some sense of long-term commitment to the countries with which they dealt. Thus, while the credit growth may have been imprudent, it came in a fairly constant stream until the 1982 crisis. Bond and share finance, on the other hand, though often channelled through banks, involves much larger numbers of investors, and has been particularly prone to speculative excess. These effects were felt through the early 1990s Latin American stockmarket booms, ended by the sudden flight of portfolio capital, most notably in the 1994–5 Mexican crisis. Bond finance can also be highly volatile, especially for Latin American countries with their record of political and economic instability. Interest charges on bonds are expressed in terms of a 'spread' or margin over the annual yield on US government securities (Treasury Bills): the higher the perceived default risk, the wider the spread. Thus, for example, between mid-1997 and late 1998 the average spread on Brazil's and Argentina's government bonds rose from about 3 per cent to about 11 per cent, partly as backwash from the East Asian financial crisis. The change was a major cause of the late-1990s growth in these countries' debt interest/export ratios (Table 2.5). A further widening of the bond spread to over 20 per cent bankrupted Argentina in 2001. For neo-structuralists and radical statists such episodes show how 'globalized' money markets are a disruptive exogenous force, able to harm Latin America through the premature financial liberalization imposed by the IMF and other international creditors (Green 1995: 85–7; ECLAC 2000: 14–30; Stallings and Peres 2000: 25–33).

However, domestic factors were clearly significant too. For example, the Chiapas uprising in Mexico that helped precipitate the 1994–5 tequila crisis came as a response to rural poverty. Mexican political uncertainties were heightened by the aura of corruption and criminality, probably involving the narcotics trade, that surrounded the PRI, the national governing party. Outside assistance was made available to help retrieve the situation. In 1995, Washington coordinated a US$50 billion international rescue package for the Mexican currency. Once again, self-interest impelled the US to support its southern neighbour. The IMF arranged loans for Brazil totalling $42 billion in 1998 and $30 billion in 2002. Argentina, in 2001, had a $48 billion credit line, cut off only after the country's political scene became hopelessly confused.

First World bond markets now discriminate sharply among Latin American debtors, inflicting harsh punishment on high levels of credit risk, but rewarding financial caution. While Brazil and Argentina have recently suffered widening interest rate spreads, the margin on Mexican and Chilean bonds has held steady at about 3 per cent. Moreover, since 2000 the US monetary authorities have cut interest rates to avert economic recession. The Treasury Bill yield, the base for bond charges, fell from about 6.5 per cent in 2000 to only 1 per cent in 2003. This contrasts with the steep rise in US interest rates imposed 20 years earlier to check inflation. So the post-1998 slackening of international financial flows has been less painful for Latin America as a whole than the 1982 debt crisis, even though certain republics, Argentina above all, are now once again in acute difficulty.

The narcotics trade

The last three decades have seen the expansion of a Latin American-based narcotics industry, stimulated by demand from the US as the primary market, though substantial deliveries are now also reaching Europe. Cultivation of the opium poppy for processing into heroin was established on a large scale in Mexico during the early 1970s, after Middle Eastern heroin consignments to North America via the 'French connection' had been disrupted by police action. Mexico also became a source of marijuana for the US. Then, in the later 1970s, the lead was taken by cocaine, manufactured from the leaves of the coca bush, a plant indigenous to the eastern foothills of the South

American Andes. The chewing of coca leaves is traditional in the Andean region, serving the Indian poor as a mild narcotic that helps them to endure hunger, thirst, and hard labour. However, consumption was static or declining until the US generated an explosive growth in demand for the more powerful derivative.

At first the extension of coca growing occurred in eastern Peru and Bolivia, while cocaine was processed for export in Colombia where, by the mid-1980s, the narcotics trade had come under the control of a few large-scale criminal gangs ('cartels') based on the cities of Medellín and Cali. As a response, Washington sought Latin American cooperation in a succession of anti-drugs campaigns, including efforts to extradite the cartel leadership for trial in the US. The cartels fought back hard against moves by the Colombian government to cooperate on extradition. Colombia suffered a wave of car bombings and political assassinations, although the most notorious gang bosses were eventually killed or captured. The US also put pressure on Peru and Bolivia to act against supply sources, with some effect. Eradication campaigns cut back the area under coca in both republics from the mid-1990s. However, cultivation shifted to Colombia where, for various reasons, control proved more difficult. Colombia began the 1990s in a comparatively strong economic position, less susceptible to Washington's leverage over debt relief and aid. Also, the country's forested mountain terrain has accommodated a long-standing leftist guerrilla insurgency, sustained by grievances over unequal landownership, and the ascendancy of two elite-dominated political parties (Chapter 5). During the 1980s, an attempt had been made at drawing the rebels away from armed struggle into electoral politics. Right-wing murder campaigns against left-wing candidates frustrated the strategy. At the same time, agrarian violence grew as drug dealers invested their profits in land, often displacing peasant cultivators. Estate owners sponsored right-wing 'paramilitary' forces to counteract guerrilla kidnapping and extortion. The price of coffee, Colombia's leading export, fell by 80 per cent between the late 1970s and early 1990s, one of the sharpest declines for a major commodity, increasing coca's attractions as an alternative crop. The presidency of Ernesto Samper (1995–8) was weakened by evidence that drug money had funded his election. So lawlessness increased further, even after the mid-1990s destruction of the Medellín and Cali cartels. Smaller-scale trafficking groups multiplied. The FARC (Revolutionary Armed Forces of Colombia), the principal left-wing guerrilla movement, gained strength by 'taxing' coca cultivation as it expanded within Colombia. A new president tried to negotiate with the FARC, granting them a demilitarized 'safe zone', but guerrilla activity continued. This made the government change course once again, with a strengthened counter-insurgency effort, from 2000 backed for the first time with substantial US aid under 'Plan Colombia'.

How should these developments be interpreted? Many observers argue that the US has inflicted severe damage on Latin America through the narcotics trade, both by acting as the primary source of demand, and by responding to the issue in a misguided fashion. Washington, the argument runs, should devote more effort to curbing US drugs consumption but, instead, puts an undue emphasis on aggressive supply control programmes. They stir up nationalist feelings within Latin America, accentuate social conflict, and discourage local cooperation against narcotics. Thus, eradication efforts may have reduced the coca acreage in Peru and Bolivia, but the crop was displaced to Colombia. Also, Peru's government during the 1990s under President Alberto Fujimori became corrupt and authoritarian, with tacit US support, ultimately bringing his downfall (Chapter 5). Bolivia's coca growers have formed militant peasant unions that play on general public distaste for US interference with a 'traditional' activity (Tullis 1995: 72, 102). These groups became a destabilizing force in national politics. In Colombia, the US worked to discredit President Samper, and may have undermined peace negotiations with the FARC. Ideological prejudice makes Washington see leftist guerrillas as an obvious threat, but take a more indulgent line towards right-wing paramilitaries, even though the latter are probably more heavily involved with drugs. It is, perhaps, the continuing paramilitary attacks, in collusion with Colombian army elements, that have made the guerrillas so reluctant to give up violence.

The 'war on drugs' had some success during the 1980s against trafficking to North America across the Caribbean. However, new marketing networks soon developed through Central America. By the early 1990s, Mexican supply routes were reckoned to account for about three-quarters of the cocaine reaching the US, along with considerable quantities of heroin and marijuana. The large population of Mexican immigrants in the US, and the greatly increased road freight volumes under NAFTA, provide convenient distribution channels. Furthermore, other foreign policy objectives have compromised US action against Latin American narcotics. The issue has often been subordinated in Washington's dealings with Mexico to the overriding priority of securing that country's political and economic stability through neoliberal reforms. Agents of the Reagan administration employed drugs traffickers as secret intermediaries to supply the Contra guerrillas fighting the Sandinistas in Nicaragua.

Successful action against drug production is more likely if returns on 'legitimate' crops can be improved by, for example, better transport links and technical advice to farmers. Critics claim that the US neglects possibilities for crop substitution in favour of coercive measures. Neoliberal economic reform may have had particularly damaging effects on smallholder agriculture by opening up domestic markets to subsidized First World produce. It has been alleged (see above) that US policy was responsible for depressing the price of coffee, a peasant staple across much of the Andean foothills and in this region often the only feasible cash crop alternative to coca.

Yet many of these points are debatable. First, it must be noted that the greatest expansion of the cocaine trade occurred during the 1980s, when Latin American output seems to have risen about three-fold, and the US retail 'street' price fell from about $500 to $150 per gram. Since then the US price has stabilized, while the US consumption volume has roughly halved. Latin American cocaine production may also have fallen, though to a much lesser extent: a greater share or output is now absorbed by non-US markets, mainly in Europe (*The Economist* 2000, 2001: 11). All this suggests that the drugs boom was partly supply-driven, and that control programmes have had some effect. Washington has made significant attempts at limiting national demand. During the 1990s, the US prison population doubled, exceeding two million, with most of the increase coming through narcotics convictions. It cannot yet be judged whether current strategies for Latin American supply control are likely to prove useful over the long term. Eradication drives certainly reduced coca output in Peru and Bolivia, though with politically damaging side effects whose full significance is, so far, unclear. Colombia has only just begun the intensive aerial herbicide spraying of land under coca, backed with extra military spending to combat the guerrilla threat. The country's coca acreage fell by an estimated 30 per cent in 2002 (*The Economist* 2003a). Perhaps recent terrorist outrages here have brought public acceptance of a stronger security effort, as happened earlier in Peru.

How far have anti-drug programmes been at fault in neglecting crop substitution? The criticisms made on this point seem over-stated. US-backed schemes have focused on the coercive aspect, but the same does not hold with other funding sources. About 70 per cent of the quite considerable aid inflows reaching Peru and Bolivia in the 1990s was provided by Western Europe and Japan for general economic purposes. During this period, Peru and Bolivia achieved unusually rapid agricultural output growth (World Bank 2001b: 194–6, 348–53). As we have seen, Washington was not mainly responsible for low coffee prices. Furthermore, the strength of the drugs economy is partly a consequence of Latin America's own agrarian inequality and development failure. Cultivation and processing are carried on with a good chance of escaping detection in the region's under-policed frontier zones, where settlement has been promoted as part of misconceived ISI strategies (Chapter 8). Coca growers have responded to eradication drives by moving to more remote parts of Amazonia. Marijuana and opium poppies are grown in deep ravines, to escape aerial surveillance and herbicide spraying. Poor standards of public administration have weakened even well-financed crop substitution projects, leaving peasants without the necessary technical advice and inputs. While coca bushes will flourish on infertile hillsides, legitimate crops require better quality land, from which poor settlers have commonly been excluded by their inability to bribe the officials responsible for its allocation (Morales 1989: 57).

What impact has the drugs trade had on Latin America's general economic performance? The business might, perhaps, be seen as useful to the region, providing an unusually buoyant source of export revenue. However, studies of the subject put most emphasis on the harm done (Morales; Tullis). Addiction has become more widespread in producer countries. It is suggested that foreign currency earnings from narcotics have put upward pressure on inflation and real exchange rates, weakening legitimate exports, which are also at risk from the trade sanctions threatened by the US against countries deemed to be insufficiently vigorous allies in the war on drugs (Sheahan 1987: 284). Coca growing, subject to displacement by eradication drives, is a cause of deforestation. Soil and rivers have been poisoned by the sulphuric acid and other chemical wastes from processing sites. Above all, drug trafficking has further weakened state power by aggravating criminality and violence. This last effect is clearest in Colombia, relatively unscathed by the 1980s debt crisis, where output growth declined sharply after 1990, against the regional trend (Table 2.1). The political assassinations that heightened Mexico's 1994–5 crisis (Chapter 3) apparently involved drug money.

Nevertheless, the damaging effects of the drugs trade should not be exaggerated. Despite its widening ramifications, the business is still heavily concentrated on a few countries (Colombia, Peru, Bolivia,

Mexico), where in each case it was reckoned by the mid-1990s to account for about 3–5 per cent of national income and a fifth of export earnings, proportions which must subsequently have diminished, except for Colombia. Coca only grows well in certain parts of Amazonia. There has been some increase in local narcotics consumption, though so far on a rather modest scale by US standards. Alcohol abuse remains a much more serious Latin American problem (Tullis 1995: 49–54). The domineering figures characteristic of the drugs industry in its boom phase, for example Pablo Escobar in Colombia, Roberto Suarez in Bolivia, and the Arellano brothers in Mexico, have passed from the scene by death or capture. The more atomized trafficking structure that has replaced them is proving unable to subvert the higher levels of government, something that once seemed a real possibility.

Conclusion

External forces have not been the primary cause of Latin America's difficulties since 1945. US intervention and influence have only had decisive effects in some of the smaller Caribbean basin republics. Elsewhere, the relationship between changing US official attitudes and the course of Latin American politics has remained rather loose. Washington cannot bear much responsibility for the deficiencies of the region's governments. US trade policies have, on the whole, been helpful to Latin America, with Cuba an important exception. The growth of foreign debt resulted mainly from economic strategies determined within Latin America, and international creditors exercised some restraint when enforcing their claims. The Latin American drugs trade was fostered by chronic rural poverty and state weakness, as well as US demand. Therefore, it seems that the fundamental obstacles to achieving sustained development in Latin America should be sought in the region's own social and political characteristics. These are the concern of the next chapter.

5   Society and politics

Latin American society in 1945 was still mainly rural and agriculturally based, with about 30 per cent of the population living in towns, a figure that had risen to 70 per cent by the 1990s. Compared with the larger East Asian NICs, Latin American urbanization levels were already relatively high in the 1940s, while the subsequent population shift into cities and out of farming occurred at a slightly less rapid pace. However, Latin America's most distinctive social feature has been unusually marked income inequalities between rich and poor (Table 5.1). During the oligarchical period such disparities were based on elite control over government, large landed estates, and coercive labour recruitment methods. This chapter first discusses why Latin American inequality has persisted, or perhaps even grown wider, despite the decline of agriculture's relative economic importance and some enlargement of political participation. We then examine the features of Latin American politics that have caused endemic government weakness and instability.

Table 5.1 Income inequality, *c.*1975 (% share of household income, by percentile group of households)

		Poorest 20%	Richest 10%
Argentina	1970	4.4	35.2
Brazil	1972	2.0	50.6
Mexico	1977	2.9	40.6
South Korea	1976	5.7	27.5
United Kingdom	1979	7.0	23.4
US	1980	5.3	23.3

Source: World Bank 1987: 253.

Rural society

The distribution of Latin American landownership, established by the early twentieth century, was grossly unequal. A small minority of large holdings had become overwhelmingly predominant. (For example, in Mexico at the outbreak of the 1910–20 revolution *haciendas* held 90 per cent of the country's farm land.) Individual properties extended over several hundreds or even thousands of acres, occupying the most fertile, well-watered tracts, with the best access to markets. Most of the rural population were either poor peasants, supporting themselves from marginal smallholdings, perhaps supplemented by occasional wage work, or lived on the estates as a resident labour force, often allocated subsistence plots under servile tenancies.

Until the late 1950s, this agrarian structure continued essentially unchanged, except for the weakening of the *haciendas* that occurred after revolution in Mexico and Bolivia (1952). Latin American populism denounced the estates as archaic survivals. ECLA analysis claimed that their failure to provide the food required by rapidly growing urban populations was a major cause of inflation. Nevertheless, political circumstances (see below) deterred governments from trying to remedy the maldistribution of landholding, until the 1959 Cuban revolution and growing difficulties with ISI gave the issue a new urgency. During the 1960s and 1970s several agrarian reforms were launched, but they had little or no effect in reducing rural income inequality. Schemes were often targeted against underused estates and 'feudal' practices, so owners could react to the threat of expropriation by adopting more mechanized techniques, evicting labour tenants, and converting them into a casual work force. Large estates often profited from government efforts to strengthen the balance of payments by technical support and subsidized credit for new export crops: cotton and sugar in Central America, or soya beans as an alternative to coffee in Brazil. In Peru, nationalized *haciendas* became producer cooperatives, whose permanent employees benefited at the expense of temporary, 'outside' workers. Elsewhere, as in Chile, land redistribution favoured a restricted middle class of capitalist farmers (Sheahan 1987: 130–54).

Some attempts were made at upgrading peasant agriculture through 'integrated rural development' projects, which relied on intensive, small-scale farming methods and village cooperation. Most programmes of this type failed through mismanagement, underfunding, bureaucratic infighting between rival agencies, and the inferiority of the land at the peasants' disposal. Government agronomists took a patronizing, racially prejudiced attitude towards the people they were assigned to help. (Distinct rural Indian populations, defined by language, dress, and ethnicity, remain in Guatemala, Ecuador, Peru, Bolivia, and parts of Mexico. Many of Brazil's rural poor are of African descent.) Where Indian identity had dissolved into the general *mestizo* culture, the usual case over most of Hispanic America, there was still likely to be a marked lack of sympathy between relatively prosperous, educated, light-skinned *técnicos* and mainly illiterate peasants. Also, small farmers' earnings were held down by price controls on basic foodstuffs imposed for the benefit of urban consumers (de Janvry 1981; Bethell 1994a: 360–85). As a contrast, in South Korea and Taiwan the comprehensive agrarian reforms undertaken during the 1950s established egalitarian patterns of landownership, while well organized government technical support raised farmers' incomes and eliminated rural poverty.

Urbanization

Latin America's rural income inequalities have been reproduced in the towns. Between the 1940s and the 1970s the region's urban population grew at an annual average rate of 4–5 per cent (doubling every 15–20 years), with about 40 per cent of the increase coming through migration from rural areas. More recently, there has been some decline in the rate of urban growth, and in the contribution made to it by rural emigration. Migrants have been both 'pushed' from the countryside by landlessness, poverty, and underemployment, and 'pulled' to the cities by the attractions of urban life. ISI offered new employment opportunities, together with improved education, health care, and other social provision, all concentrated in the major towns (Gilbert 1994: 23–56).

However, although the number of industrial workers grew quite rapidly, the share of the labour force employed in industry remained relatively low, only about 20–25 per cent on average by the 1980s (compared with 30–40 per cent in the leading East Asian NICs). The difference resulted from Latin America's limited success in developing manufactured exports, and from a premature emphasis within the region on labour-saving technology.

The MNCs may have been one cause of the labour-saving bias (Chapter 3), but it was reinforced by other influences. Managers in both national and foreign-owned firms aimed at high levels of automation to counteract what was perceived as insufficient skill and motivation among factory-floor operatives. Employment opportunities were also limited by the improved pay and conditions secured through trade union pressure in the larger establishments. Habits of labour militancy had been introduced to Latin America from Europe and the US during the early twentieth century. Certain key groups – railwaymen, dockers, and miners, for example – found that their capacity to halt the flow of exports gave them considerable leverage. The first strikes provoked harsh repressive measures but, as time passed, more subtle techniques of containment evolved, through officially recognized trade unions, arbitrated pay settlements, minimum wages laws, job security, and social welfare benefits for those workers who had political influence and a significant disruptive potential. Even where trade unions developed under government sponsorship and control, as in Mexico or Brazil, their members' acquiescence was bought at the price of substantially increased labour costs, another inducement for employers to adopt capital-intensive, high-productivity methods (Banuri 1991:171–220; Bethell 1994b: 307–57).

Thus, job opportunities in industry were limited, and there was a more rapid growth of employment in the service or 'tertiary' sector. Economic development requires more service workers (shop assistants, teachers, architects, doctors, government functionaries, etc.). However, by East Asian or First World standards Latin American service sector employment accounts for an unusually high share (about 60 per cent) of the urban labour force. It includes many street vendors, shoeblacks, rubbish collectors, and others in precarious occupations. These elements are commonly described as the informal sector, a rather elastic term, embracing a wide range of low-income workers, either self-employed, or employed by others, for example in the small 'sweat shop' factories that larger firms often use as subcontractors, to evade trade unions, minimum wage laws, and other welfare requirements. The informal sector comprises 25–40 per cent of the labour force in Latin American cities, and has been the main means of livelihood for recent migrants from the countryside.

Immigrant and informal sector workers commonly show great resilience under adverse conditions. They have not constituted a marginal underclass, demoralized by a fatalistic 'culture of poverty', as anticipated by some observers in the 1950s (Roberts 1995: 158–61, 189–94). Many individuals have progressed to more rewarding occupations, or at least secured education and upward mobility for their children. Most newcomers soon relinquish rural ties and assimilate to city life. Temporary urban residence with alternating, 'circular' migration between town and country, a common habit in Africa and South Asia, is quite unimportant in Latin America.

Nevertheless, even during the period of rapid economic growth up to the early 1980s, the earning capacity of the urban poor was held down by their limited skills, by the limited opportunities for better-paid formal sector work, and by competition from the continuing influx of rural immigrants. The self-employed were liable to official harassment, especially when operating at or beyond the margins of legality. Small-scale businesses suffered exploitation from their suppliers, and restricted access to credit (Bethell 1994a: 276–7, 299–304; Gilbert 1994: 39–71).

Some neoliberals have suggested that cutting back the tangled mass of corruptly administered regulations which underpin the formal/ informal sector divide would allow small enterprises to flourish and put economic development on a more healthy basis (Gilbert 1994: 71–3). Despite the publicity given to this argument, it has not yet been implemented with any vigour, or yielded any substantial results. Since the onset of the debt crisis, low-grade service activities have multiplied further, as a refuge for people affected by falling real wages, cuts in social spending, and the loss of formal sector employment. The urban poor have borne the main brunt of austerity measures. The upper classes, on the other hand, have fared comparatively well: the high interest yields on financial assets required by stabilization programmes and the investment income from holdings of flight capital have compensated for the decline in business profits (Bethell 1994a: 307–12).

Latin American urban geography reflects and reinforces income inequality. The speed at which urbanization occurred put severe pressure on the housing stock, populist rent control laws discouraged private investors from building accommodation to lease out, and governments proved capable of meeting only a small part of the demand for shelter. Most public sector housing catered for a privileged minority of state employees. Therefore, the urban poor resorted to self-built squatter settlements, usually on land occupied through collective invasions, or through illicit purchases that violated planning regulations. Such 'shanty town' development has come to house 30–60 per cent of the population in Latin America's major cities. Governments eradicated particular squatter settlements but, on the whole, tolerated the phenomenon, as an apparently low-cost expedient, as a way of securing electoral support, and as a safeguard against social discontent. It was hoped that settlers who built and improved their own houses, sometimes to quite high standards, would be diverted from radical politics (Gilbert 1994: 79–101).

Plate 5.1 Caracas, Venezuela, 1978: shanty town suburbs and city centre
  skyscrapers (Michael Freeman/Corbis)

All this contrasts with the East Asian NICs, where squatter settlements are strictly controlled and a large part of the urban population
is housed in government schemes. They have been more successful
here because of greater state autonomy and administrative efficiency.
Also, more of the labour force works in capitalist manufacturing or
other formal sector employment and, thus, can meet rent or mortgage
payments from a regular wage. Most East Asian public housing projects consist of multi-storey apartment blocks. Therefore, the region's
major cities are relatively compact, while in Latin America the mass
of self-built settlement, rarely more than one or two storeys high, has
produced low-density sprawl (Plate 5.1).

Latin America's pattern of extensive urban growth entails serious
economic disadvantages, though some authors have seen it as a
convenient, if inequitable, way to make cheap labour available for
capitalist employers (Abel and Lewis 1993: 112–13). Much squatter
settlement property remains without legal title, and is thus unaccept-
able security for bank loans, another obstacle to informal sector
business success. The provision of water, sewerage, and electricity is
costly. Buses rather than rail systems (the more efficient alternative)
must serve as the main form of public transport. Labour productivity
suffers because of time-consuming, exhausting journeys to work,

which average 90 minutes in big Latin American cities, compared with 30–45 minutes in their East Asian counterparts. Reliance on long-distance motor vehicle commuting makes transport costs a considerable item in Latin American urban household budgets, and a politically sensitive issue. Governments have held down fuel prices, and then been forced to raise them under austerity programmes, by eliminating subsidies, or imposing new taxes. Rioting against higher bus fares has disrupted several attempts at economic stabilization (Ward 1990: 92–113; Gilbert 1994: 113–19, 146–9).

Politics since the 1940s: general trends and special cases

Each Latin American country has its own distinctive political history. However, the most common pattern followed over the last half century included a phase of competitive electoral democracy, subject to occasional military intervention. The period lasted from the 1940s to the 1960s. Then dissatisfaction with erratic civilian rule made the military take power on a longer-term basis. Military dictatorship gave way to a process of redemocratization in the 1980s.

Some countries do not fit this scheme. In Mexico a single party, the PRI, held power continuously until the late 1990s as legatee of the 1910–20 revolution, by reinforcing a populist/nationalist appeal with electoral fraud and pervasive patronage networks. Venezuela was controlled by a succession of military dictators until the late 1950s when, after the fall of General Pérez Jiménez, civilian politicians reached an understanding among themselves to guard against the return of authoritarian rule. Subsequently, buoyant tax revenues from the country's oil industry funded the political system. While the presidency alternated between the two main parties, their supporters shared access to employment in the proliferating state bureaucracy. The armed forces were kept content with generous pay and equipment grants. The wider electorate benefited from welfare and development programmes.

Colombia's politics has been shaped by the long ascendancy of two rival parties, the Liberals and the Conservatives. There is a tradition of rural violence, dating back to nineteenth-century conflicts, and fostered by the country's rugged geography. Both Liberals and Conservatives have continued under elite leadership, drawing support from across a wide social range. After an episode of civil war and dictatorship in the 1950s the two parties formed a coalition government which agreed on a pragmatic, moderate approach to development issues. ISI was combined with export promotion, balance of payments deficits were contained, and the foreign debt remained modest (Sheahan 1987: 275–88).

Other special cases include Costa Rica, where a comparatively egalitarian pattern of landownership limited social conflict. Costa Rica abolished its army in 1949, and democracy has survived without interruption ever since. However, old-style landed oligarchies dominated the country's Central American neighbours until the 1970s. In Paraguay, even more backward and 'feudal', the personal autocracy of General Alfredo Stroessner held sway from 1954 to 1989. Cuba's position as the world's largest sugar exporter gave the island a period of relative prosperity in the 1940s, when alternative supply sources were disrupted, followed by economic stagnation when competition resumed. The rigidities of the sugar monoculture, and Cuba's dependence on the US as an export market, prevented development through ISI. Nationalist aspirations were frustrated. The rule of the dictator Batista was marked by cynicism, lethargy, and incompetence, so in 1959 Fidel Castro and his small guerrilla band could sweep to power from their rural base. Castro soon nationalized all US and other foreign investments, committing Cuba to socialism in alliance with the Soviet Union. His regime has survived into the twenty-first century (Wynia 1990: 287–307; Appendix 1: Biographies).

Through all this variety of detail a common failure to maintain viable development strategies affected every regime type. Electoral competition brought chronic political instability and executive weakness. Despite their attempts at 'autonomy', military dictatorships proved susceptible to vested interests and popular dissatisfaction. In Mexico the PRI's long monopoly of power made administrative corruption deeply ingrained. Venezuela's arrangements gave an appearance of democratic moderation, but frittered away the country's oil wealth. Colombia's two-party consensus blocked agrarian reform and perpetuated high levels of income inequality. The radical left was pushed into armed opposition, aggravating habits of rural lawlessness, and helping to lay the basis for the country's involvement with the international drugs trade (Chapter 4). On Cuba, socialism brought some gains in general welfare, together with extreme economic inefficiency.

Civilian democracies 1940s–1960s

From the 1940s to the 1960s the larger republics usually had elected civilian regimes. Voting rights were extended to most of the adult population. The landed oligarchies' predominance was a thing of the past, and governments responded to the demands from urban interests by promoting ISI. However, for various reasons, the new balance of social forces proved highly unstable, and policy implementation suffered as a result.

First, the big landowners had not been eliminated. They could offer a significant challenge to the urban-based populist movements that gained ground during the period. In their early years, populist coalitions brought together affluent business and professional people (often referred to as the bourgeoisie) with the lower middle classes and manual workers. These allies cooperated to end exclusive oligarchical rule, but once that objective had been achieved, they soon found reasons for disagreeing among themselves. Workers sought higher wages and welfare benefits. The bourgeoisie took fright at labour militancy and the threat of redistributive taxation, issues on which common cause could be made with elite landowners. Many landowning families proved adaptable. Their members developed interests in manufacturing, commerce, and banking. They entered the higher levels of government service. Successful businessmen from lower-class or immigrant backgrounds could become assimilated to older forms of wealth through marriage alliances and the purchase of estates. Long-standing Latin American customs of highly personalized social relations, based on clientelism and *compadrazgo* (ritual kinship), facilitated the intermingling of landed and urban elites (Wynia 1990: 47–56; Cubitt 1995: 103–6, 179–86; Roberts 1995: 60–9).

One economic result was that much private sector ISI manufacturing came under the control of a few closely knit oligopolies, their position reinforced by connections with well-placed state officials. Tariff barriers limited competition from imported goods. Collusion between firms to fix prices and share out government favours limited competition within protected domestic markets. The high levels of business profits that resulted helped to perpetuate extreme income inequality. Industrialists had little need to make their factories more efficient.

Habits of partiality, inefficiency, and corruption in public administration represented another inheritance from the past, with very damaging consequences after 1945 as state functions were enlarged to implement ISI. Latin American traditions of administrative weakness were first established during the colonial period, when both the Spanish and Portuguese monarchies failed to maintain effective control of their distant overseas possessions. Creole elites penetrated the government apparatus as a source of power, prestige, and income. Post-independence *caudillos* habitually used public appointments to reward friends and followers. The multiplication of superfluous government jobs, allocated to poorly qualified candidates on a patronage basis, became a standard means by which twentieth-century populist politicians sought middle-class votes (Williamson 1992: 374–6; Bethell 1994b: 9–20, 33–55).

Latin American constitutional arrangements followed the US model. Presidents chosen through a national vote held executive power, alongside two-chamber legislatures whose members represented local and regional constituencies. The redrawing of constituency boundaries lagged behind the population shift to the cities, so there was a persistent over-representation of rural areas, where estate owners remained influential, through customary techniques of patronage and intimidation. Also, the Catholic Church still gave strong support to hierarchical values, especially in the countryside. Often the presidency was held by a populist, elected on a narrow majority or plurality, drawing support mainly from urban workers, and obliged to deal with a legislature where his conservative opponents had a strong presence. The conflicts and stalemates that resulted were aggravated by the weakness of party structures. Most populist leaders relied, above all, on charismatic mass appeal. Their parties amounted to little more than personal vehicles, lacking organization or continuity (Bethell 1994b: 108–29).

Furthermore, civilian governments were subject to military interference. Latin America's armed forces asserted or reasserted a political role in the early 1930s, when they helped to oust export oligarchies weakened by the international economic depression. Since the later nineteenth century military training had become increasingly rigorous, to cope with the technical demands of modern warfare, allowing more men from lower- or middle-class backgrounds to gain promotion as officers. They held the traditional landowning elites in low esteem, and favoured industrialization, not least because it would provide a basis for national armaments production (Rouquié 1987: 84–92). But the value which military men placed on discipline made them exasperated at the confusion of civilian politics, and tempted them to intervene as moderators with the aim of restoring stability, by annulling elections or displacing a particular president. So political leaders in office were deterred from risking unpopularity by taking a firm line on contentious issues while opposition parties were encouraged to be intransigent and obstructive, in the hope of provoking military action from which they might benefit.

Governments could not raise taxes to match the growth of spending on development projects, social welfare, and bureaucracy. It also proved impossible to control inflation, correct exchange rate overvaluation, improve administrative standards, tackle the issue of land reform, or check shanty town settlement. Although politicians used strongly nationalist rhetoric to rally support, maintaining the pace of ISI came to depend on MNC investment. However, when it seemed that budget deficits and inflation were becoming unmanageable, foreign capital inflows ceased. Economic growth came to a halt; political confusion and popular unrest intensified. The military then decided, with considerable civilian approval, that the imminent threat of social breakdown required them to retrieve the situation by taking power into their own hands. The course of events in Brazil between 1950 and 1964, under presidents Vargas, Kubitschek, Quadros, and Goulart, illustrates this common sequence (Wynia 1990: 219–33). Argentina experienced similar stresses during the 1946–55 presidencies of Juan Perón (Appendix 1: Biographies).

Military dictatorships 1960s–1980s

Military regimes often began by acting more decisively than their civilian predecessors, for example in undertaking land reform (Peru, Ecuador), or in raising extra taxes to correct budget deficits and restore investors' confidence (Brazil, Argentina). Yet, sooner or later, every country under military rule suffered a recurrence, in aggravated form, of the macroeconomic imbalances that had characterized populist, civilian ISI. The 1980s debt crisis came as a result.

First, authoritarian governments made very little progress in eliminating personalism, clientelism and corruption from business and state administration (Evans 1979: 101–62). Failure on this point occurred partly because the attitudes involved were so deeply rooted. Also, reform would have to be imposed on upper-class social groups which the military hoped to keep as allies against the radical left. The armed forces did not have a sufficient range of expertise within their own ranks to staff the enterprises and agencies involved in the development effort, establishing a suitably professional, technocratic mentality. For example, the continued influence of economic elites made the Brazilian military regime build its economic strategy round an indiscriminate, wasteful system of subsidies, biased towards large-scale enterprises, and increasingly reliant during the 1970s on foreign borrowing (Frieden 1991:118–25). Business lobbyists obstructed proposals to improve efficiency by exposing national industry to more competition through lower import duties. An excessive emphasis was still given to the production of motor cars and other consumer durables for the middle class.

Military regimes also became susceptible to pressures 'from below'. During the 1960s and 1970s some attempts were made to follow the Cuban model of rural-based insurrection elsewhere in the region, but they succeeded only in Nicaragua. Here, the Sandinistas could overthrow the Somoza regime because its narrow, selfish character, effectively rule by a single family, had alienated every level of society, including the urban middle and upper classes. Otherwise, rural rebellions were contained. Governments took note of Batista's downfall, strengthened their security forces, with US backing, and made sure that insurgents did not succeed by default, as had happened on Cuba. Repressive measures were also sufficient to deal with the various clandestine urban guerrilla movements (Green 1991: 122–31; Bethell 1994b: 198–214, 438–68).

The main popular challenges to authoritarianism took other forms, including upsurges of labour unrest. The trade unions built up under state patronage in the populist period were subjected by the military to strict and, on the whole, effective control. However, a more aggressive 'new unionism' appeared, concentrated among younger workers in the recently established or enlarged automobile and engineering industries. The 1969 *cordobazo*, a wave of strikes and rioting by car workers and university students in the Argentine city of Córdoba, struck a fatal blow against General Onganía's regime, allowing the populist Juan Perón to briefly regain power (Skidmore and Smith 2001: 94–7; Appendix 1: Biographies). During the later 1970s the Brazilian military government was weakened by strikes in the motor vehicle factories of the São Paulo region (Bethell 1994b: 357–67; Cubitt 1995: 187–8).

Mass activism extended further with the 'new social movements' (NSMs), neighbourhood associations by which poor people sought to improve their condition through a mixture of self-help and pressure on government for better services. The NSMs provided a means of giving expression to popular discontent when the electoral process was suspended. They were most conspicuous in the shanty towns of the big cities, and received encouragement from the Catholic Church, radicalized under the influence of Liberation Theology (Gilbert 1994: 142–3; Cubitt 1995: 85–7, 194–9). Growing agitation on material issues became linked with demands for a return to democracy. This deterred governments from imposing austerity measures to correct the widening balance of payments deficits caused by the 1970s oil price increases. Reliance was put on foreign borrowing instead (Banuri 1991: 21–4).

The military regimes' basic weakness lay in their lack of sufficient legitimacy. Despite the *caudillo* tradition, and various attempts to establish quasi-fascist ideologies, the assumption prevailed that Latin America's colonial origins and the nineteenth-century independence movements made the region part of a 'western civilization' in which political pluralism and representative institutions have become the norm. Even the export oligarchies had practised representative government, though with very limited participation. The armed forces claimed that their superior professionalism gave them the right to take charge of national affairs, but only on a temporary basis, as an emergency measure, 'a state of exception'. Bureaucratic authoritarianism intended to restore democracy in a healthier, 'purified' form, an objective which required that account be taken of public opinion, and which complicated the pursuit of development goals (Rouquié 1987: 330–69). In the East Asian NICs, on the other hand, traditions of political mobilization were comparatively weak, and democracy was an alien principle that had not yet put down deep roots, leaving governments with a freer hand to conduct policy on strictly technocratic lines (Gereffi and Wyman 1990: 139–204; Haggard 1990: 126–60).

Chile provides the one notable exception to the Latin American record of weakness and failure under military rule. During the 1950s and 1960s the country had experienced the usual problems of political instability and unviable ISI, culminating in 1970–3 with Salvador Allende's socialist government and its overthrow by a military coup. The initial results of the undiscriminating neoliberal policies followed by General Pinochet's regime after 1973 were unfavourable (Chapter 3), and by 1982 the country laboured under a heavy debt burden. However, since then Chile has made a strong recovery by developing new export lines. The 'non-traditional' export growth owes a good deal to abundant natural resources, but they have been reinforced by an unusually high degree of coherence in policy execution. While the basic strategy of raising efficiency through neoliberal measures continued, the errors of the 1973–82 period were recognized, and much more attention was paid to maintaining a stable, competitive REER. Difficult adjustments had to be made at every level of society. Industrialists lost tariff protection. Industrial workers suffered lay-offs and wage cuts. The big landed estates expropriated under Allende were not reconstituted. But structural reform was pursued long enough to prove its worth. For example, in agriculture, medium-sized farms became dominant, their operators imbued with a stronger entrepreneurial spirit, and capable of supplying foreign markets (Hojman 1993; Collins and Lear 1995).

The effectiveness of the Pinochet dictatorship resulted from special circumstances. Chile's public administration has relatively high standards of competence and honesty. Most of the country's population is concentrated within a few hundred miles of the capital city, reducing the need for the patronage techniques associated elsewhere with regionalist tendencies and weak central control. The armed forces enjoy a certain prestige as guardians of the national territory against hostile neighbours, Argentina in particular. Above all, the 1973 coup apparently saved the middle class from socialist revolution, so Pinochet attracted a significant personal following, which enabled him to weather the debt crisis and continue as president until 1989, giving his technocratic advisers a free hand (Frieden 1991:174–7). In Chile the neoliberal approach was apparently justified by results. Since 1990 it has been continued by elected politicians with some adjustments along neo-structuralist lines.

Politics since the debt crisis

As for the ISI period it remains difficult to generalize about Latin American politics because the details of national history vary widely, though certain broad themes can be discerned. The most notable trend during the 1980s was the shift back from military dictatorship to elected civilian government. However, some countries did not fit this pattern because they had previously avoided or escaped military rule. These variant cases include Mexico, Venezuela, Colombia, and Costa Rica. Cuba's post-1959 communist dictatorship persisted under Fidel Castro. Comment on Latin America's political development since the debt crisis has gone through two main phases, the first running up to the early or mid-1990s, the second covering subsequent years. In the first phase, the overall impression drawn was fairly optimistic, at least from the perspective of those who favour neoliberal capitalism; during the second, the outlook has become much more clouded and uncertain. This section reviews the sources of first-phase optimism and second-phase doubts, for the light they may cast on Latin American prospects. An attempt to judge very recent events must, of course, be speculative.

When the Latin American debt crisis began many observers thought that economic recession would soon provoke widespread civil disturbance and intensified political conflict, perhaps leading to upheavals of a revolutionary character. These expectations proved unfounded. The military regimes gave up office, peacefully on the whole, and by the early 1990s every country in the region except Cuba had a civilian government based on an election of some kind, even if in many cases the level of authentic democratic participation was questionable (Green 1991: 103–6). Furthermore, all governments, again except Cuba's, were committed with varying degrees of enthusiasm to neoliberal economic reforms. Voters, in general, favoured centrist or centre-right presidential candidates. The performance in nationwide elections of left-wing politicians and parties, advocating a socialist or populist approach, was relatively weak (Appendix 2: Chronology).

The new strength of electoral democracy came partly from the way that the experience of holding state power left military men, Chile's perhaps excepted, thoroughly chastened by the disappointing results from their stewardship, with no wish to keep responsibility for intractable national problems. The civilian politicians who took over, however unsuccessful in economic management, at least got credit for restoring personal liberties. Traumatic memories remained of the human rights abuses committed under military rule. Few civilians would still consider inviting military intervention, as had happened so often in the past. Developments elsewhere gave support to the liberal-democratic cause. During the 1980s both Spain and Portugal consolidated parliamentary institutions after several decades of dictatorship, challenging the view hitherto current on the Latin American right that democracy was somehow alien to the Iberian heritage (Williamson 1992: 375–7). International communism ceased to represent a plausible threat or provide justification for military coups. Nicaragua's radical Sandinista government, which had taken power after the overthrow of the Somoza regime, was voted from office in 1990. This change, together with the loss of Cuban backing, helped bring an end to left-wing guerrilla movements in El Salvador and Guatemala.

In certain cases electorates came to support, or at least tolerate, economic liberalization. They did so because of the failure of statist alternatives, as demonstrated by the collapse of Soviet communism, by Latin America's own debt crisis, and by the rampant hyperinflation generated by various 'heterodox' policy experiments attempted in the region during the later 1980s (Chapter 3). Chile's strong economic recovery from 1984 apparently showed the value of the neoliberal approach. The return of large-scale capital inflows to Latin America after 1990 made possible rapid consumption gains. In 1994–5 Carlos

Menem was re-elected president of Argentina, Alberto Fujimori was re-elected president of Peru, and Fernando Henrique Cardoso was elected president of Brazil, largely on the strength of their success against inflation, and in Fujimori's case a commitment to fighting left-wing terrorism. They secured popular mandates to continue neoliberal stabilization measures. Both Menem and Fujimori won re-election despite showing a clear taste for unscrupulous, authoritarian methods. Both had practised neoliberalism 'by surprise' during their first presidential terms, embarking on free market reforms which completely contradicted populist election campaign rhetoric (Stokes 2001; Appendix 1: Biographies, for Menem).

However, from the later 1990s, in some though not all Latin American countries, the neoliberal cause lost momentum; chronic government weakness and instability re-emerged. Here, we note some examples of intensified political strife, setting them beside cases of relative stability. How should these differing outcomes be explained, and which pattern is most likely to prevail across the region? Undoubtedly, conflict has grown, above all, through disappointment with the results of neoliberalism: the losses suffered by particular groups, even when average income per head rose quite strongly, often the case for a time in the early 1990s; the general economic slow-down that set in after the tequila and East Asian crises; and the abuses which came to be associated with free market measures, privatization especially.

The experience of two second-term presidents is illustrative. Both Menem and Fujimori lost public support almost immediately after re-election, yet both sought a third term. In pursuit of this objective Menem increased government spending and debt; he also split his Peronist party. Argentina's 2001–2 crisis came largely as a result (Chapter 3; Appendix 1: Biographies). Fujimori secured re-election in 2000 through blatant fraud. Popular protest soon drove him from office, bringing to power an inept successor without a party base. The Fujimori regime's systemic corruption was revealed, discrediting much of the political class. In other republics no commanding figure prevailed long enough to push forward decisively the neoliberal cause. Venezuela's Carlos Andrés Pérez began his presidency in 1989 with an attempt at reform by surprise. The anti-austerity riots that followed claimed several hundred lives. He was impeached on corruption charges in 1993. The next president to be elected also reversed policy after striking a populist pose. Disgust at these betrayals gave an overwhelming victory in the 1998 presidential election to Hugo Chávez, an ex-paratroop officer who had led abortive coup attempts against the Pérez administration (Buxton and Phillips 1999b: 162–84). Chávez's bombastic, confrontational style soon antagonized all except a loyalist minority concentrated among the urban poor, provoking capital flight and strikes that crippled the oil industry, Venezuela's export staple, in 2002–3. In Ecuador and Bolivia a series of weak coalition governments failed to maintain a consistent reform line. There were six different holders of Ecuador's presidency between 1996 and 2000. Both countries have relatively large indigenous elements (about 70 per cent of the population in Bolivia, 40 per cent in Ecuador) which took an increasingly active political role from the late 1980s. A new Indian militancy developed here partly as a reaction against neoliberal measures favouring large-scale capitalist landholding, export agriculture, timber extraction, oil drilling, and mining projects. Post-modernist doctrines of grassroots consciousness gave ideological support. The mobile phones made available through economic liberalization helped to coordinate protest, especially the road blocks which became a favourite technique of direct action (Wiarda and Kline 2000: 331–67; Vanden and Prevost 2002: 78, 87–96). In Colombia, rural guerrillas and drug-related violence have become extremely disruptive (Chapter 4). Taken together, such cases suggest movement towards a general crisis of the Latin American state. 'By the late 1990s Latin America's economic, social and political problems had reached explosive proportions' (Keen and Haynes 2000: 578).

Nevertheless, a balance must be struck with counter-examples that cover about two-thirds of the region's population. In Chile the centre-left Concertación alliance has held power continuously since 1990, and the closest electoral challenge comes from right-wing parties, themselves moving towards the middle ground. Over the same period politics have become more settled and consensual in the Central American republics. In Mexico, the PRI finally relinquished its hold on government at the 2000 presidential election. However, the victor was Vincente Fox of the right-wing PAN, committed to continuing financial restraint and free market policy. The leftist PRD's candidate took just 17 per cent of the vote. Lula da Silva of the left-wing PT (Workers' Party) was elected to the Brazilian presidency in 2002, but only after toning down his radicalism.

One characteristic shared by nearly all these 'stabilizing' countries is a relatively favourable economic context; most are post-1990 'fast growers' (Table 3.1), while intense political conflict usually accompanies the persistent stagnation or decline of output per head. Thus the Concertación governments in Chile have benefited from the foundations for prosperity laid during the Pinochet years. Close proximity to the US has helped Mexico and Central America, through export opportunities, migrant worker remittances and, in certain cases, substantial aid flows. Washington used its aid leverage with particular force on Honduras and Nicaragua to ensure that they persevered with neoliberalism. Brazil's large size and comparatively flexible, diversified economic structure eased the liberalization process. For Argentina, on the other hand, giving up ISI entailed particularly severe adjustments (Chapter 3). Venezuela, heavily reliant on petroleum exports, suffered a massive terms of trade shock through the post-1980 oil price decline. Argentina and Venezuela are the only major Latin American countries where income inequality rose during both the 1980s and 1990s (Vanden and Prevost 2002: 102–3). Ecuador also lost oil revenue. Bolivia's tin exports collapsed. Oversupply in the world coffee market hit Colombia, a major grower, aggravating rural poverty and the disruptive effects of the narcotics trade.

Apart from the economic background, political institutions and personalities may have an independent significance. Some countries were more fortunate than others in their leading public figures. Thus, Brazil got as president Fernando Henrique Cardoso, a man of great distinction, quite unlike Argentina's Carlos Menem (Appendix 1: Biographies). Venezuela's collusive two-party system became especially corrupt during the ISI period, and the country had no recent experience of military rule. So revulsion against the established order made voters here put their faith in Lieutenant-Colonel Chávez, going back to the *caudillo* tradition. In Mexico, on the other hand, the ruling elite had developed a comprehensive structure of control through the PRI. The party apparatus, embracing urban government, client trade unions, and *ejido* peasant landholding collectives, was able to manage the social tensions generated by free market reform. The 1994 Chiapas Indian uprising remained a local affair. Unlike Ecuador and Bolivia, Mexico's indigenous people are only a small minority (about 12 per cent of the population), and their grievances could not have a decisive impact. Furthermore, the PRI's upper ranks came to be dominated by highly educated technocrats, many with post-graduate degrees from US universities, who understood the need for democratic concessions and set aside the authoritarian instincts of the 'dinosaur' party old guard. Electoral procedures were adjusted in ways calculated to favour the pro-business PAN over the populist PRD. Reform let the PAN advance by stages, winning state governorships which prepared the way for its success at national level in 2000 (Wiarda and Kline 2000: 384–99).

Plate 5.2 Democratic handover in Brazil, 2002: President Cardoso (left)
 greets his newly elected successor, Lula da Silva (AFP/Corbis)

Lula da Silva's qualified acceptance of neoliberalism and 2002
election victory in Brazil represent another notable transition (Plate
5.2). He agreed with senior PT colleagues to shift his stance after
losing three successive presidential races (1989, 1994, 1998) on a
populist platform. One of 22 children of an illiterate farm worker, da
Silva had become a factory mechanic, an activist in the late 1970s
car workers' strikes that helped undermine the military dictatorship,
and then leader of the PT as it grew from the new labour movement.
He served a long, hard apprenticeship to reach power, training him
in the arts of compromise and, unlike Hugo Chávez, is not just a
vacuous demagogue. At the time of writing, da Silva seems determined to hold his government on a moderate course and curb the
PT's militants. Brazil and Mexico, Latin America's two most important countries, therefore, have a fair chance of maintaining political
stability. This, however, may require faster national income growth
and help from a buoyant world economy, conditions which are by no
means certain (Chapter 9).

Conclusion

Latin American society is characterized by unusually marked income differences between rich and poor, a feature that originated in patterns of racial stratification and highly unequal landownership first established during the colonial period. Inequality was perpetuated under twentieth-century ISI by continuing rural poverty, formal/informal sector occupational divisions in the cities, together with the resilience and adaptability shown by national elites. The various regimes that held power between the 1940s and the 1980s lacked sufficient strength and stability to pursue effective economic programmes. Chile has, perhaps, recently escaped from the syndrome of social conflict and development failure, but it is still uncertain whether the country can provide a model for the rest of the region. Chile completed the most painful early stages of restructuring under authoritarian military rule. Elsewhere, the attempt was made at combining democratic politics with neoliberal measures which have, as yet, brought little material benefit to the population at large. Public impatience and discontent grew during the 1990s, though whether this presages a general return of chronic political instability is, so far, unclear. Whatever the case, many observers came to believe that better social welfare provision must play a key role in consolidating democracy and free market reform.

6 Social welfare

So far we have usually taken as our criterion of national development the output of goods and services per head of population, clearly
an inadequate guide to welfare standards. Social welfare cannot be
measured with any precision, but one commonly used index is infant
mortality, the death rate among children less than one year old
(Sheahan 1987: 24–7; Abel and Lewis 1993: 33–47). Various other
more elaborate 'human development' or 'physical quality of life'
indices have been devised, combining infant mortality with literacy,
the incidence of gender discrimination, and so forth, but they do not
produce substantially different results (Cubitt 1995: 20–3).

Figure 6.1 relates infant mortality and GDP per head for various
Latin American and East Asian countries in 1980. (As a comparison,
in that year the United Kingdom's GDP per head was about
US$13,000 and its infant mortality rate stood at 12 per thousand.)
Higher levels of output per head are associated with lower infant mortality, but the relationship is not very close. For example, in 1980
China and Bolivia had a similar GNP per head, but China's infant
mortality was much lower. Between Chile and Brazil there was an
equivalent discrepancy. Judged in this way China and Chile, together
with South Korea and Cuba, may be said to have a relatively good
welfare performance, while the record of most Latin American countries is much weaker.

It is also useful to consider changes over time (Figure 6.2). All
Latin American countries have experienced a long-term fall in infant
mortality, but at varying rates, which do not entirely correspond to
economic conditions. Thus, Chile achieved an unusually rapid infant
mortality reduction during the 1970s and early 1980s, when the pace
of economic growth was very slow. Over Latin America as a whole,
infant mortality continued to decline during the 1980s and 1990s,
despite the economic stresses resulting from the debt crisis. There has

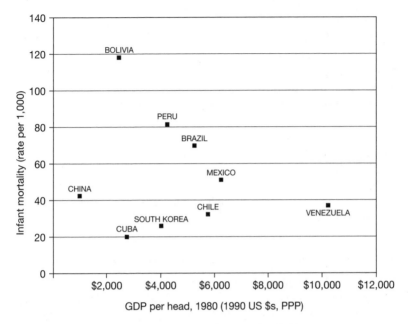

Figure 6.1 Infant mortality* relative to GDP per head, 1980

Sources: World Bank 2001b; Maddison 2001.

Note: *Annual deaths per 1,000 among infants aged 0–1 year.

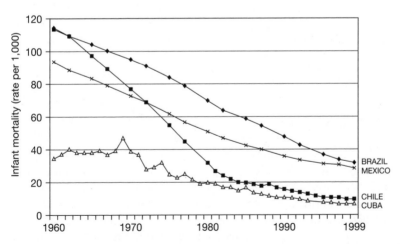

Figure 6.2 Trends in infant mortality, 1960–99

Source: World Bank 2001b.

also been some recent improvement in education enrolment rates (see p. 106, Table 6.1).

So, while Latin America has made significant gains in social welfare, the standards reached have been rather modest relative to the region's levels of output per head. The shortfall is undesirable in itself and has contributed to economic difficulties. Poor health, nutrition, and education have impaired workers' productive efficiency (Maddison *et al.* 1992: 51–2). On a number of occasions, for example in Brazil during the 1970s, unsatisfactory welfare indicators weakened government authority and led to the pursuit of unsustainable spending programmes. The improvement of Latin American social conditions has been limited both by the persistently high levels of income inequality, already discussed in Chapter 5, and by the particular forms that welfare provision has taken, the main concern of this chapter.

Welfare provision: origins and development

Latin American welfare services have come to deploy quite substantial resources. On average, in the region, government social spending absorbs about 10 per cent of GNP, less than in the developed countries where the corresponding figure is about 25 per cent, but more than in other parts of the Third World. In the East Asian NICs the share taken is only about 5–7 per cent. Two-thirds of East Asian social spending goes to education. Latin America puts more emphasis on health and on social security income maintenance payments (pensions, etc.), categories which overlap and will be discussed together (World Bank 1991: 66, 225; Maddison *et al.*1992: 109, 205). Education is dealt with separately.

Latin America's distinctive budgetary pattern originated in the early twentieth century when the Southern Cone countries began extending retirement pensions to a wider range of occupational groups. Hitherto, such benefits had been confined to a privileged minority of state functionaries: high-ranking military, judges, and other senior officials. Additional pension funds were now established for other groups that showed themselves capable of political or industrial militancy, often including bank clerks, railway and oil industry employees in the first instance, followed by other formal sector urban workers. Coverage reached the urban informal sector and the countryside much more slowly, if at all. As time passed, other countries embarked on the same course, Brazil in the 1930s, Mexico in the 1940s. Retirement pensions were supplemented by health insurance, maternity allowances, unemployment, sickness, invalidity, and child benefits (Maddison *et al.* 1992: 96–101, 191–3). This piecemeal enlargement of welfare, to coopt or buy off potential opposition is sometimes referred to as 'Bismarckian', after the German chancellor who pioneered the technique in the later ninteenth century (Abel and Lewis 1993: 3–6). Latin American populist politicians favoured the approach as a relatively cheap way to secure electoral support and social cohesion, minimizing the conflict between capital and labour associated with industrialization. More conservative opinion, including the Catholic Church, approved of welfare as reinforcing family life, considered to be under threat from secularism and economic change.

Latin American social security developed in a selective fashion, based on occupation-specific insurance schemes. Priority was given to relatively privileged groups, reflecting and reinforcing established income inequalities. This contrasts with the approach taken in Britain, the US, and most other developed countries, where universal benefits were financed from general government revenues, including progressive income tax paid at higher rates by the rich, redistributing purchasing power to the poor. In continental Europe, where practice originally evolved along 'Bismarckian' lines, welfare provision became effectively universal and redistributive by the mid-twentieth century.

Latin American welfare systems have had many weaknesses. First, provision has been highly discriminatory and stratified, with the most generous benefits received by the more affluent, and the least help going to those with the greatest need. In the 1970s, about 40 per cent of the region's population still lacked any insurance cover, and remained dependent on residual public health services (Abel and Lewis 1993: 49–74). For example, the Mexican government's health spending per head for state employees, beneficiaries of the ISSTE insurance fund, was nearly twice that for private sector employees under the inferior IMSS scheme, and 20 times greater than for the uninsured population (Maddison *et al.* 1992: 202). There was a marked urban bias in the distribution of services. Within the cities, hospitals and clinics were disproportionately concentrated at central locations, so that poorer people living in irregular suburban settlements commonly resorted to private treatment at their own expense, even when they had insurance, because of the long journeys required to attend state facilities (Ward 1990: 155–67).

Apart from the inequality of provision, the methods used to finance Latin American social security have also had many undesirable features. Schemes were usually funded in the first instance partly by employees' contributions and partly by payroll charges on employers. Employees' contributions could often be set against income tax liability, a feature that was most useful to the higher paid. Payroll levies gained favour in Latin America partly because they were relatively easy to collect, an important consideration for countries with weakly developed administrative structures. Also, charges which fell on capitalist enterprises, many of them foreign-owned, were more politically acceptable than taxes paid by the wider public.

By the 1970s, social security contributions were typically adding 50 per cent to the wage bill of large-scale Latin American businesses, impairing export competitiveness, encouraging the use of labour-saving technology, and limiting the growth of formal sector employment. For example, cane-cutting machines had been adopted on Peru's coastal sugar estates as a response to the unionization of the labour force and the introduction of social security arrangements (Abel and Lewis 1993: 160–1). Under ISI many large firms with a monopoly or near-monopoly position in their protected national markets could pass on extra payroll costs by charging higher prices. This outcome was likely to be regressive, bearing heavily on poorer consumers with little or no welfare coverage who financed benefits received by the more affluent.

Usually pension and other social security schemes were first set up on a 'funded' basis. It was intended that participants' contributions should be invested in productive assets, generating an income stream from which future obligations could be met. ECLA economists justified welfare provision as a means of generating capital for development projects. But, as time passed, surpluses were eroded by the growing number of claimants, and by the granting of excessively generous benefits, in response to political pressures. Many employees in higher-grade occupations became entitled to retire on full pay in their forties or fifties, after as little as 20 years' service. They could then take up another well-paid job, perhaps leading to another pension. The most privileged workers, those who could retire earliest, tended to have the longest life expectancy and so put the heaviest burden on pension funds. Social security institutions rarely succeeded in building up an investment stock to match the multiplying demands placed upon them. Pension contributions were used to subsidize medical services. Reserves suffered depletion through being lent to governments at low rates of interest that did not keep pace with inflation. In Argentina, social security income covered mounting losses on the railways, most of them formerly British-owned, after they were brought under state control by Perón during the late 1940s. The network was used to create jobs for Perón's trade union supporters, and soon became grossly overmanned (Abel and Lewis 1993: 187–95).

Thus, instead of being funded, an instrument for raising national savings rates, Latin American social security became 'pay as you go', with current income used to meet current outgoings. Many schemes went into deficit as contributions lagged behind the growth of entitlements. Governments then felt obliged to meet shortfalls by inflationary finance (printing money), and by general taxation that fell most heavily on the poor. To the extent that welfare provision offered, or seemed to offer, a guaranteed income, people may have been discouraged from building up their own savings for emergencies and old age. In East Asia, the comparative weakness of democratic pressures allowed governments to keep social security outlays at minimal levels. Some neoliberals argue that this has been an important cause of the region's unusually high rates of personal or household savings, and its limited reliance on foreign capital.'

Finally, the profusion of occupation-specific schemes raised administrative costs. For example, 35 distinct social security funds were established in Chile; Cuba before the 1959 revolution had more than 50. Individual funds developed their own hospital networks, distinct from, and greatly superior to the services maintained by national ministries of health for those without insurance. So, there was much duplicated investment, and a low occupancy rate in many of the best facilities, from which the uninsured population was excluded. The channelling of resources towards occupational schemes encouraged an emphasis on curative medicine and the neglect of preventive public health measures, such as mass screening or immunization campaigns. Nomination to appointments in welfare bureaucracies served as a widely used form of political patronage. Administrations became noted for their opulent head office buildings and generous salary scales. In Latin America, management costs absorbed 10–15 per cent of social security expenditure, compared with the norm of 3 per cent or less found in developed countries (Edwards 1995: 269–72).

Some of the authoritarian military governments that took power during the 1960s and 1970s tried to put social security on a more coherent basis. Brazil's post-1964 regime unified provision for private sector workers, eliminating the separate occupational funds with their trade union representation on management boards. Coverage was extended to a much larger share of the labour force, including rural workers. The aims were to cut administrative costs, legitimize military rule, and end the use of social security schemes as a trade union power base. Bringing in extra contributors would raise the national savings rate. In practice, however, benefit levels remained grossly unequal, while the reliance on regressive payroll taxes and the shift towards curative treatment at the expense of public health measures continued. Public hospitals were unable to meet the growth of demand, and the contracting out of services to private clinics resulted in large-scale overcharging and fraud, for the benefit of a powerful 'medico-pharmaceutical complex'. When party politics resumed under the *abertura* of the later 1970s, clientelism and patron-age superseded technocratic rationality in appointments to the social security bureaucracy. The economic crisis of the 1980s plunged the whole system into deficit (Abel and Lewis 1993: 341–64; Maddison *et al.* 1992: 96–101).

On Cuba, the post-1959 revolutionary government pursued a vigor-ous programme for improving welfare by redistributive measures on behalf of the poor, replacing stratified occupational funds with a comprehensive benefit system, and extending health services into rural areas. The effects of these changes in reducing malnutrition and infant mortality have attracted admiration (Cubitt 1995: 95–6). However, at the time of the revolution conditions here were already quite favourable. An abundance of good-quality farm land suitable for sugar growing, combined with ready access to North Ameri-can markets, capital, and technology, had given Cuba one of Latin America's highest levels of income per head, and a relatively low infant mortality rate. Unequal property ownership and chronic un-employment outside the months of the sugar cane harvest limited the benefits reaching agricultural workers, but popular living standards were still well above the regional norm. After 1959, the US trade embargo, mismanaged attempts at economic diversification, and the loss of labour discipline associated with the transition from capital-ism to socialism, all took their toll. In the late 1970s, the island's output per head was no higher than it had been 20 years before (Sheahan 1987: 45–7, 246). (For Latin America as a whole output per head rose 70 per cent over the same period.) A third of Cuba's doctors left the country during the first three years following the revolution, as part of a larger middle-class exodus. These circum-stances held back welfare gains. A detailed demographic study suggests that only about a quarter of the eleven-year increase in life expectancy at birth which occurred in Cuba between 1953 and 1970 is attributable to the revolution (Díaz-Briquets 1983: 120–5).

Welfare since the debt crisis

What effects have the debt crisis and the subsequent shift towards neoliberal economic policies had on Latin American welfare? During the 1980s an average decline of about 5 per cent in regional income per head was accompanied by widening inequality. The rich were, to an extent, insulated from recession through the revenues on their holdings of flight capital, payable in foreign currency and thus not curtailed by exchange devaluations. Since 1982, creditors have usually enjoyed high real interest rates. On the other hand, urban formal sector real wages commonly fell by 20 or 30 per cent. Price levels were pushed up by devaluations and by the elimination of consumer subsidies to cut fiscal deficits. Unemployment rose. Social programmes were curtailed as foreign debt service payments took a growing share of government budgets (Abel and Lewis 1993: 75–107; Bulmer-Thomas 1994: 400–3). Economic growth resumed in the 1990s, but the recovery was brief and did not improve income distribution.

Some authors, therefore, argue that a severe deterioration in general well-being has occurred. 'Health, nutrition, infant mortality, educational enrolment and food consumption have all suffered' (Abel and Lewis 1993: 96). 'Rising health problems are clearly related to the present economic crisis. ... Latin American infant mortality rates declined in the 1970s but increased in the 1980s as a result of deteriorating economic conditions' (Keen and Haynes 2000: 581–3). 'Although [by 1998] the rich had had a vintage decade, most of the region's people were poorer and more insecure; their homes, communities, schools and hospitals were collapsing around them' (Buxton and Phillips 1999a: 29). In fact, however, matters are not so clear-cut. Most Latin Americans certainly suffered declining income per head during the 1980s, but at the same time improvements in infant mortality (Figure 6.2) and other social indicators continued. For example, life expectancy at birth, the best measure of general mortality, rose about 5 per cent in Latin America between 1980 and 1990, a rather smaller gain than for the 1970s, but very similar to the East Asian experience over that period. The deceleration of the fall in mortality continued after 1990, despite Latin America's output per head recovery (Table 6.1). The reasons for the discrepancies between economic and demographic trends are not yet fully understood, so here we can only mention various possible explanations.

It is sometimes implied that declining Latin American mortality does not reflect general welfare conditions because it came, above all, through new low-cost technology, in particular cheaper vaccines

Table 6.1 Life expectancy, mortality, and immunization in Latin America and East Asia, 1970–99

| | Life expectancy at birth (years) | | | | Decline of mortality (%) | | % of children immunized* | |
| | | | | | Child (0–5) | Adult (15–60) | | |
	1970	1980	1990	1999	1980–99	1980–99	1980	1999
Latin America	60.5	64.6	68.0	69.8	52	16	39	88
East Asia	59.3	64.7	67.5	69.1	46	22	48	82

Source: World Bank 2001b.

Note: *Against measles, diphtheria, whooping cough, and tetanus.

for immunization against childhood diseases (Buxton and Phillips 1999a: 26–7). Such medical advances have clearly been important, but should not be over-emphasized. Since 1980, Latin America's immunization coverage has grown only a little faster than East Asia's. Also, Latin American adult mortality rates have fallen significantly (Table 6.1).

The harm done to welfare by austerity and liberalization programmes was mitigated by the fact that they had their most severe effect on employees in government and ISI industries. These urban formal sector workers had previously received incomes quite considerably above the subsistence margin, and so could maintain nutritional standards, despite falling wages, by curtailing non-food expenditures. There is some evidence for dietary deterioration immediately after the onset of the debt crisis, but by 1990 food supplies per head in most countries matched the levels current ten years earlier (Goodman and Redclift 1991: 65–7; FAO 1995: 233–6). The average incidence of malnutrition, as measured by the proportion of underweight children, held steady at about 10 per cent (World Bank 2001b). Most of the poorest Latin Americans are still in agriculture which, at least during the 1980s, was comparatively resilient, especially where opportunities remained for frontier colonization, and where illicit drugs production could flourish (Chapters 4 and 8; Bethell 1994a: 386–7). International migration, mainly to the US, has been an important means of relief from adversity in Mexico and the Caribbean basin.

Within Latin American cities, the decline of formal sector employment and wage rates was offset to some extent by the compensatory growth of the unrecorded informal economy. More married women have taken up street trading and similar activities, to supplement household budgets. The spread of contraception and falling birth rates have helped women's entry to the paid labour force (Chapter 7). The fertility decline, itself, improved infants' survival chances.

As previously noticed, the share of government social spending in GDP was cut from about 11 per cent to about 10 per cent between the early 1980s and early 1990s, a less severe reduction than for some other budget categories, before recovering to about 13 per cent (Stallings and Peres 2000: 66). The effects of this increase reached public sector health provision, which claimed some 3 per cent of GDP (Table 6.2), a relatively high level by the standards of East Asia and other developing areas.

Health standards could continue to rise in Latin America during the 1980s, despite recession and curtailed public expenditure, on the basis of investments begun before the debt crisis in facilities and in the training of medical personnel. Even when economies were made after 1982 by neglecting capital maintenance and by allowing inflation to erode health workers' real salary level, the stock of professional expertise was still usually maintained (Maddison *et al.* 1992: 201–2). The number of physicians per thousand people in the region rose from 0.7 in 1970 to 1.1 in 1984 and 1.4 in 1990 (World Bank 2001b). Conversely, however, much of the 1990s health spending growth went on restoring pay rates and replacing worn out equipment. In Argentina, at least, child mortality was cut by the improved water quality brought through the privatization of urban utilities (*The Economist* 2003b).

Table 6.2 Health spending in Latin America and East Asia, 1990–9

	1990–4				1995–9			
	Public sector (%)[a]	Private sector (%)[a]	Total (%)[a]	Total per head[b]	Public sector (%)[a]	Private sector (%)[a]	Total (%)[a]	Total per head[b]
Latin America	2.7	3.2	5.9	362	3.2	3.2	6.4	437
East Asia	1.8	2.0	3.8	87	1.9	2.2	4.1	156

Source: World Bank 2001b.

Note: a As a % of GDP; b PPP $s.

Health and welfare may also have been affected by changes in methods of social service delivery. The main steps taken on this point included attempts to direct expenditure in a more precise, selective fashion. For example, until the early 1980s the Mexican government maintained general food subsidies, much of the benefits from which went to relatively affluent consumers, while low-income peasant farmers were obliged to sell their crops at controlled prices. The cost of government subsidies on basic products had reached 10 per cent of GNP (Abel and Lewis 1993: 120). After 1982, these arrangements were replaced by a more economical system of subsidized food rations targeted at poor families. Other examples of selective spending include the Emergency Social Fund set up in 1986 by the Bolivian government to alleviate the distress resulting from austerity measures, and Mexico's Solidarity Programme (Maddison *et al.*1992: 203–4; Gilbert 1994: 151–3). These schemes bypassed established bureaucracies and were supposed to enlist local community cooperation, with the aim of minimizing implementation costs and maximizing benefits to the poor.

The fashion for targeting and selectivity in provision was combined with measures decentralizing welfare administration, handing over responsibilities to local and private sector agencies. The trend drew support from a broad range of opinion, including both neoliberals and their post-modernist critics, reflecting the widespread agreement reached that central government, at least under Latin American conditions, has a natural tendency to become bureaucratic, patronage-ridden, and corrupt. Localized bodies, it was hoped, would be more accountable to the public and, therefore, more effective.

Schemes for decentralized provision often put much emphasis on popular participation through local community action, of the type made conspicuous by the new social movements (NSMs) that proliferated in Latin America from the 1970s (Chapter 5). NSMs demanded better government services, but there was often also a strong commitment to self-help. For example, shanty town neighbours might work together on building a health clinic, extending a school, paving streets, or laying water pipes, perhaps using materials provided by state agencies. Such initiatives have received a good deal of support from NGOs (non-governmental organizations) or PVOs (private voluntary organizations, the equivalent US expression), terms now commonly applied to a wide range of non-official bodies. While most NGOs operate on a small-scale, local basis, some are national or international in scope. As well as the thousands which have appeared in Latin America and other developing regions,

there are large numbers based in the developed countries but concerned with the Third World, for example Oxfam, Care, and Save
the Children.

NGOs rely on voluntary support, but also employ paid, full-time
specialists (lawyers, doctors, engineers, architects, etc.). During Latin
America's period of military rule professionals and academics
excluded for political reasons from government or university posts
often found work in the NGO sector. The Roman Catholic Church's
engagement with social issues under the influence of Liberation
Theology (Chapter 5) provided another important source of leadership. Because of their perceived flexibility, moral commitment, and
capacity for liaising with poor people through small-scale projects,
NGOs came to attract a good deal of international development aid,
and often served as vehicles for targeted social spending by Latin
American governments.

Chile, under the Pinochet dictatorship, provided the earliest and
most notable example of a neoliberal assault on centralized public
welfare, though the reforms here had an autocratic tone and made
little use of NGOs. Resources were shifted away from hospitals
in the major cities to more widely dispersed primary health care
clinics under local municipal control, committed to the delivery of
preventive measures such as immunization and education in basic
hygiene. Targeted programmes distributed food to pregnant women
and young children (World Bank 1990: 85; Gilbert 1994: 151). Major
cost savings were made, because less was spent on elaborate equipment, and because pay rates for medical staff were lower in the
municipal sector than in the unionized central government facilities.
The Pinochet regime could override hitherto powerful professional
vested interests and pressure groups. Chileans got the right to opt out
of the state health service and contribute instead to private sector
medical insurance plans (Isapres). Neoliberal opinion held that more
competition among providers would help raise efficiency. Other Latin
American countries began similar experiments in the 1990s.

The Pinochet measures did ensure that a notable infant mortality
decline continued (Figure 6.2), despite a very severe economic crisis
in the early 1980s, and the fact that Chile had already achieved almost
complete immunization coverage by the start of the decade. In
Mexico, targeted social funds were, perhaps, helpful for managing
popular discontent and negotiating the shift to political pluralism.
There are cases elsewhere, in Venezuela for example, of devolved
government undertaking useful initiatives (Tulchin and Garland 2000:
218). During the second Cardoso presidency in Brazil (1999–2002)

selective poverty relief schemes made some progress. But, on the whole, health and welfare service reforms seem to have brought little benefit, perpetuating or aggravating inequalities of provision. In Chile, the Isapres sought affluent, low-risk contributors, at the expense of the public sector insurance fund (World Bank 1993: 162). The mortality trend here is still quite favourable, but probably mainly as a result of strong economic growth from the mid-1980s, and large increases in government outlays on health after the return to democracy in 1990. The results of other and more recent experiments with private sector medicine are equally unimpressive (Abel and Lewis 2002: 172–88).

Public service devolution often disadvantages poorer districts by increasing their dependence on a meagre local tax base. Many NGO and community-based projects have disappointed. Only a small minority of the poor, rarely more than 10 per cent in urban areas, involve themselves with neighbourhood associations. Participation is limited by the daily struggle to make a living and care for children. Economic and occupational differences between households restrict any sense of collective identity (Gilbert 1994: 130–1). The economic crisis of the 1980s, it is suggested, has increased residential mobility and community fragmentation, leaving individual or family action as the main element in survival strategies (Bethell 1994a: 311–12). The NGOs' effectiveness has been further impaired by the hostility of state bureaucracies, poor coordination, political factionalism, and attempts to impose middle-class ideological preoccupations on poorer clients (Abel and Lewis 1993: 421–37).

Pension provision is another aspect of social policy that has attracted considerable attention. As noticed earlier, state pensions systems were originally established on a funded basis, partly with a view to generating capital for development but, over time, populist pressures made them 'pay as you go' and often insolvent. Chile's military dictatorship pioneered pensions reform in the late 1970s by introducing a new system of privately managed funds (AFPs) to replace the established state schemes. The restructuring eliminated employers' payments, seen as a burden on business enterprise. Participating employees' future pension rights were related more strictly to contributions made, with the aim of avoiding deficits and generating surpluses. It was hoped that competition between funds to attract participants by offering the most favourable returns would improve administrative efficiency. Also, fund managers would pay closer attention to the quality of investments made, ensuring that assets were used productively and not depleted through wasteful state spending, in the way that previously had happened so often (Collins and Lear 1995: 167–81).

During the later 1980s, Chile's national savings rate grew quite strongly, a development which neoliberal observers thought resulted, at least in part, from the new AFP system. So, many other Latin American countries began imitating the Chilean pensions policy, encouraged by the World Bank and IMF. However, as with health service reform, so far the results are mediocre. Since 1990, savings rates have fallen across most of the region (Table 3.1, column 13). Pensions reform in its early stages has done nothing to check the trend, and has been a major cause of recent rises in budget deficits. Payments to public sector superannuation funds are reduced, while the state is left to support those who have already reached retirement age. This 'transition cost' puts a severe burden on government finances (Mesa-Lago 2002). It now seems that Chile's 1980s savings growth came not through the AFPs, but through a resurgence of corporate profits, on the strength of the commodities export boom and the dictatorship's pro-business stance. (For example, state enterprises were sold off very cheaply.) When Chile returned to democracy, government became less helpful to corporate enterprise, economic growth slowed, and the national savings rate fell.

Education

Latin America's public education systems have grown substantially since the early twentieth century and, in principle at least, expansion occurred on an egalitarian, universalist basis, contrasting with the stratified approach taken for health and social security services. Education was seen as an instrument to secure national unity, integrating immigrant and indigenous Indian populations. This required comprehensive coverage under central control. By the 1940s, most Latin American countries had made school attendance compulsory and free for young children. By 1960, high levels of primary school enrolment had been reached (Table 6.3) and about two-thirds of the adult population was reported as literate. Educational trends in the East Asian NICs up to that date appear broadly similar.

However, Latin American education showed serious qualitative defects, with frequent pupil absences, dropping out, and grade repetition, especially at the primary level. By 1980, the proportion of Latin American children completing the four years of basic education

Table 6.3 Proportions of age groups enrolled in education, 1960–97 (%)

	Primary education*			Secondary education			Higher education		
	1960	1980	1997	1960	1980	1997	1965	1980	1997
Brazil	95	98	125	11	34	62	2	11	15
Mexico	80	120	114	11	49	64	4	14	16
Chile	109	109	101	24	53	75	6	12	32
South Korea	94	110	94	27	78	102	6	15	65

Source: World Bank 2001b.

Note: *Enrolment rates in excess of 100 per cent occur when older children attend primary school.

considered necessary to acquire functional literacy was still only about 60 per cent. Such problems resulted partly from variations between schools in expenditure levels. Much of the revenue for basic educational services was raised locally, to the detriment of standards in rural areas with a limited taxable capacity. Ethnic, linguistic, and class differences impaired teachers' communication with their pupils. In the East Asian NICs, on the other hand, education benefited from the greater degree of cultural uniformity. Higher population densities made it easier to enforce compulsory attendance laws, and ensure that young children had access to schools of a viable size. So, good-quality primary schooling was established here by the 1950s, providing a much better basis than in Latin America for the subsequent growth of secondary education. Latin America then suffered during the 1960s and 1970s from a disproportionate, lavishly funded expansion of university education, undertaken in response to pressure from the higher income groups, and mainly for their benefit. The university sector came to take about 40 per cent of state education spending in the region (compared with 10–20 per cent in East Asia), at the expense of primary and secondary schools (ECLAC 1992: 37–61).

The effects of the debt crisis and its aftermath on Latin American education have been the subject of extravagant assertion by authors hostile to neoliberalism. 'As a result of sharp cuts in educational budgets, education levels throughout the area have declined' (Keen and Haynes 2000: 583). It is suggested that spending per child fell by as much as 28 per cent during the 1980s (Buxton and Phillips 1999a: 26), and that economic recession made more children drop out of school so that they could work and contribute to hard-pressed family budgets (Gilbert 1994: 77). In fact, the slow rise in enrolment rates has continued, now concentrated at the secondary level (Table 6.3). The proportion of pupils completing four primary school years has grown from about 60 per cent to about 80 per cent over the last two decades. The trend may be partly 'inertial'. Previous educational expansion raised the proportion of parents who have had some schooling themselves, and who therefore want their own children to remain at school. Also, recession reduced the employment available for children, and the opportunity cost of keeping them out of the labour market (ECLAC 1992: 41). Intensified competition for job opportunities increased the importance attached to educational qualifications (Roberts 1995: 130). Lower birth rates cut the share of school-age children in the population. Average spending per student fell by about 10 per cent during the 1980s, mainly through a decline in teachers' real pay, and fully recovered in the 1990s. Like health budgets, Latin American public expenditure on education still claims a share of national income (about 4 per cent) that is relatively large by East Asian standards (World Bank 2001b: 80).

Once again, however, underlying social inequalities and class bias in provision still make Latin American outlays rather inefficient, and not much has been done to correct this weakness. Chile offers the most notable example of neoliberal education reform. The Pinochet regime imposed unusually severe cuts on the educational budget, mainly affecting the university sector, and gave elementary schooling a higher priority. Public universities were obliged to cover most of their costs from tuition fees. Private institutions, operating on a commercial basis, were allowed greater freedom to compete for students and state funds. The aim was to raise efficiency and promote more vocationally oriented teaching. A voucher subsidy scheme also encouraged private sector elementary and secondary schools. Public school administration was decentralized, depriving employees of civil service status, and making it easier to dismiss incompetent teachers. The post-1990 democratic government restored public sector teachers' labour privileges, and established a comprehensive national testing system. These various changes have been followed by what is, in Latin American terms, a relatively strong growth of the tertiary-level enrolment rate (Table 6.3). However, the trend seems to result, above all, from middle-class prosperity and the benefits secured by children at the better-quality private schools. Across the school system as a whole attainment remains low by international standards, and shows little sign of improving (Abel and Lewis 2002: 273–5, 285–300). Elsewhere in Latin America reform measures have been even less effective. While some progress has occurred, the region's educational disadvantage relative to East Asia and the developed countries persists.

Conclusion

Latin American welfare standards have risen, but the advance has been limited by the bias of state services towards the relatively affluent. Occupationally stratified insurance schemes developed during the ISI period for better-paid formal sector workers took a large share of spending, at the expense of public health measures and primary education. Although the 1980s debt crisis brought reductions in real income for much of the population, infant and general mortality, important welfare indicators, continued to decline. The trend apparently results from better medical techniques and the fact that, for the most part, health services were maintained despite the recession. During the 1990s, economic recovery was accompanied by quite substantial increases in social welfare expenditure. However, it seems doubtful whether such increases were particularly useful for securing political and economic stability. As noted earlier, there is no clear relationship between the growth of GDP per head and of welfare outlays (Chapter 3; Table 3.1, column 15). Little has been done to improve the targeting of benefits on the poor. Enlarged social budgets became an important cause of rising Latin American fiscal deficits during the later 1990s, especially in certain 'slow growth' republics, for example Colombia and Bolivia. Pension reform has not raised savings rates in the way expected by neoliberals. Also, Latin American educational standards still give serious cause for concern, and without more rapid advance in this area a strong economic recovery is unlikely. On general welfare provision, the effects of NGO schemes and collective action among the poor seem limited. The postmodernist left has probably exaggerated the benefits likely to come from grassroots initiatives.

7 Women

In Latin America, as everywhere else, women's status is inferior to that of men. Many accounts note how gender relations in the region have been shaped by the notion of *machismo*, an attitude among men that puts an exaggerated emphasis on masculine power and virility. The mentality is believed to have originated from medieval Iberian traditions of chivalry and militarism, reinforced by the process of transatlantic colonial conquest. Support for this interpretation comes from the fact that within Latin America *macho* values are least pronounced among those indigenous populations that have kept the greatest measure of autonomy from external influences. *Machismo* sanctions male aggression and assertiveness, the 'double standard' of sexual behaviour (chastity and fidelity required of women but not men), and female exclusion from the public sphere. At the same time, *marianismo*, an ethos of female spirituality, resignation, humility, and fortitude, derived from the Roman Catholic Church's cult of the Virgin Mary, is said to have allowed Latin American women some influence at home (Green 1991: 139–40; Skidmore and Smith 2001: 62–3). However, it is doubtful whether Latin American views on gender have differed much from the patriarchal, chauvinistic male attitudes long familiar in the developed countries. *Machismo/ marianismo* never entailed the rigorous female seclusion and subjection found in much of South Asia and the Islamic Middle East. Women's life expectancy and educational attainments compare more favourably with those of men in Latin America than in other Third World regions (Table 7.1). We must also take note of Latin American women's increased participation in the labour force, their declining fertility, and the changes in their political role that have occurred during the course of the twentieth century.

Table 7.1 Male/female differentials in life expectancy and education, 1965–99

| | Female life expectancy at birth as a % of male | | | Females in education per 100 males | | | | | |
| | | | | Primary | | | Secondary | | |
	1965	1988	1999	1965	1987	1992	1965	1987	1992
Latin America	107	109	109	95	96	95	77	110	104
East Asia	106	99	106	n.a.	84	89	50	71	78
South Asia	98	100	102	54	n.a.	73	34	n.a.	56
Sub-Saharan Africa	105	106	104	56	77	81	36	59	72
Middle East	n.a.	n.a.	103	70	n.a.	83	88	n.a.	79
Developed countries	110	108	108	95	95	95	93	100	98

Sources: World Bank 1990: 241; World Bank 1991: 267; World Bank 1995: 219; World Bank 2001b: 22.

Women in the labour force

By international standards Latin American women's labour force participation has been rather low (Table 7.2), originally because of their limited employment in agriculture. The plough cultivation and cattle ranching characteristic of the region involves tasks considered too arduous for women. Also, estate operations are often performed by gang labour. Men have been reluctant to allow their female dependents to do such work, alongside or under the authority of males from outside the household circle. In Latin America, there has been less scope for employing women on peasant family farms than, for example, in East Asia, where smallholder rice cultivation entails much transplanting and weeding labour. Estate mechanization has cut back further the role of women in Latin American agriculture, a trend offset to only a limited degree by their use in some new export lines, such as Colombia's cut flower production, and Chile's fruit growing (Bethell 1994b: 484–8).

The growth of Latin American female employment over recent decades resulting from economic development and urbanization has been concentrated in service occupations. The expansion of the middle classes enlarged the demand for domestic maidservants. Women became prominent in the urban informal sector, as street vendors and laundresses, for example. Also, females have gained

Table 7.2 Women as a proportion of the labour force, 1960–99 (%)*

	1960	1980	1999
Latin America	20	28	35
East Asia	39	43	44
South Asia	33	34	33
Sub-Saharan Africa	43	42	42
Middle East	27	24	27
Developed countries	32	38	43

Source: World Bank 2001b.

Note: *These figures do not include the unpaid domestic work undertaken by women for their own families.

ground in the formal sector, as secretaries or other subordinate clerical employees in government, commerce, and finance, as shop assistants, as teachers (mainly at the primary level), and in medicine (mainly as nurses). Women's growing access to university education has allowed them to gain higher professional status, for example as doctors and lawyers, in small but significant numbers. Women now account for about half of Latin America's service employment.

However, women's role in manufacturing industry has been quite modest. They provided roughly 20 per cent of the region's industrial labour force in 1960 and 25 per cent by 1990. The corresponding figures for the East Asian NICs are 20 per cent in 1960, and 45 per cent in 1990. Part of the difference may result from the emphasis of Latin American ISI manufacturing on 'heavy' industry (steelmaking, engineering, etc.), and the weakness of 'light' export-oriented assembly work (clothing, electronics), where in East Asia females commonly take 80–90 per cent of the jobs. But even when comparison is made on an industry-by-industry basis, Latin American women's share of employment is still relatively low. Also, certain industries have experienced a marked decline of women's employment share over time, for example, in textile factories from about 70 per cent during the early decades of the twentieth century to about 30 per cent by the 1970s.

Some authors attribute the displacement of female labour to investment in more advanced and highly automated machinery (Cubitt 1995: 117), but technical change has not had this result in East Asia. Therefore, it is more likely that the recruitment of women into Latin American manufacturing has been limited by the protective legislation on their behalf introduced during the first half of the twentieth century. Such provisions raised the cost to employers of female labour and discouraged its use. The measures included the prohibition of women from hazardous occupations, controls on women's working hours (especially the outlawing of night work by women), entitlements to paid maternity leave, the establishment of nurseries for children, and equality of pay with men doing the same tasks. These regulations were sought by unionized male workers, influenced by European socialist thought, as a defence against competition in the labour market from 'exploited' women. Populist politicians were highly sympathetic to female employment protection, an issue on which they could enlist general support. Even landowning elites welcomed regulation, as a restraint on the development of capitalist industry (Bethell 1994b: 488–99).

When the authoritarian governments of the 1960s and 1970s sought to promote capitalist development by curbing trade union rights, few attempts were made at reducing legal controls on the employment of women. The military regimes' social conservatism included the belief that 'a woman's place is at home'; they had no wish to make the mobilization of female labour an important part of their economic strategy. The 1980s brought a return to democracy and some growth in women's political influence, or at least in government expressions of concern for their interests (see below). Under these circumstances, little has been done to weaken female employment protection, despite the general fashion for economic liberalization.

It is true that the enforcement of Latin American employment laws has usually been lax, so they have only had a substantial effect on employment practice in larger, formal sector establishments. Common techniques for evasion include the dispersal of tasks among unregulated informal sector subcontractors, or the use of women as outworkers in their own homes, sewing up garments, for example. Factory workers can be frequently replaced, so that they do not qualify for the benefits available to longer-term employees. However, with subcontracting and outworking it is difficult to achieve internationally acceptable levels of standardization and quality. Economies of scale are lost. High employee turnover as a means of limiting entitlement to regulatory coverage obstructs the accumulation of work force experience and skills.

As a contrast, East Asian factories have been less affected by workplace regulation, allowing them to recruit and employ larger proportions of women, a useful competitive advantage. In East Asia, as elsewhere, the strength of patriarchal assumptions has made women, by comparison with men, more flexible and tractable as workers, tolerant of lower wage rates, and more profitable to employ for those manufacturing occupations that do not require great physical strength or long training. Institutional restraints on the employment of women have constituted one more disadvantage for Latin American industry, adding to its many other problems (Chapter 2). The disadvantage seems likely to continue. The assembly plants set up in the *maquiladora* belt along the US–Mexican border and in the Caribbean basin export processing zones, have a greater proportion of women workers than does Latin American industry as a whole, but their labour forces are less thoroughly feminized than those of similar East Asian factories. Moreover, export assembly remains a very small element in Latin American manufacturing. Thus, the growth of female employment within the region during the 1980s resulted mainly from women taking up unregulated informal sector service work, as they tried to maintain household income in the face of economic recession and the consequent decline of male earnings (Chant 1991; Roberts 1995: 128–30).

After 1959, Cuba's revolutionary government encouraged women to work outside the home, as a form of self-liberation and public service, by providing nursery schools, crèches, and public laundries. Such measures had only a limited effect. Apart from the lower proportion of domestic servants, female employment patterns on the island do not differ much from those found elsewhere in Latin America (Bethell 1994b: 493–4; Cubitt 1995: 119–21). One factor limiting Cuban women's entry to the labour market has been the need for them to spend much of their time standing in queues to obtain rationed commodities, another feature of life under socialism (Sheahan 1987: 248).

Contraception and the birth rate

Latin American birth rates have fallen over the last 40 years, broadly matching trends elsewhere (Table 7.3), and to a considerable degree representing no more than the local expression of world-wide 'modernization' processes. In the past it could often be useful to have many children, as extra labour on peasant farms, as an insurance against high infant mortality, and as a support for parents in their old age. These benefits from large families have been reduced or eliminated by economic development, urbanization, medical advances, and state social provision. Infants' survival chances have improved. Increased education has raised women's aspirations and the cost of bringing up children. New consumer durables have become available, competing for a larger share of household budgets and making the costs of child

Table 7.3 Crude birth rates, 1965–99 (births per 1,000 population)

	1965	1980	1999
Latin America	40	31	23
East Asia	39	22	18
South Asia	45	37	27
Sub-Saharan Africa	48	47	40
Middle East	48	40	26
Developed countries	20	15	12

Source: World Bank 2001b.

maintenance seem more burdensome. All these influences have been at work in Latin America, rather less powerfully than in the developed countries, but more so than in Africa, for example, where economic progress has been minimal.

Nevertheless, the pace of Latin America's fertility decline cannot be entirely explained in these terms because, during the 1960s and 1970s, the birth rate was brought down more sharply in the East Asian NICs, before they had caught up with Latin American levels of income per head, urbanization, and industrialization. An important source of difference, it seems, was national attitudes and culture, less inclined to accept population control in Latin America than in East Asia. In Latin American countries the Catholic Church and its teaching against contraception had a considerable influence, at least among the ruling circles which determined official policy. Certainly, it was out of the question for Latin American governments (except in revolutionary Cuba) to make abortion facilities as freely available as in East Asia. Furthermore, Latin American policy makers were suspicious of birth control as an 'imperialist' panacea, apparently recommended by richer countries because it offered a low-cost alternative to development aid. There was much distaste for the aggressive measures to limit population growth implemented during the 1950s by the US in Puerto Rico, its Caribbean dependency. The programme included the widespread use of the contraceptive pill, at that time a recent and untested invention.

Larger populations were widely believed to be necessary for ensuring the development of abundant natural resources, providing an adequate domestic market for ISI, and increasing national military strength. (The armed forces claimed demographic policy as their special concern.) So, while the small East Asian NICs, more obviously threatened by overpopulation, became vigorously committed to birth control from the early 1960s, Latin American governments were not persuaded of the need to restrain population growth until the later 1970s, when economic prospects were clouded by growing foreign indebtedness (World Bank 1984: 170–2, 200–1; Wynia 1990: 129–31). Since then, official policy has become more tolerant of contraception, without doing much to actively encourage it. A number of large-scale private programmes have been established to promote family planning; sterilization is the most widely used method. Another recent change which has probably contributed to the Latin American birth rate decline is the growth of women's political activism and their increased self-confidence in relations with male partners (see below). Also, the economic recession and the extra pressure on women to seek paid work has encouraged them to limit their fertility (Green 1991: 142–3; Bethell 1994a: 17–27, 48–56; Radcliffe and Westwood 1993: 192).

Women and politics

During the middle decades of the twentieth century women gained voting rights throughout Latin America, with Ecuador the first country where female suffrage was granted, in 1929, and Paraguay the last, in 1961. The concession was made following the European and North American examples, as part of the wider democratic challenge to the traditional oligarchic order. The same influences also prompted efforts to improve female education, taken as a sign of modernity and progress. Educated women, it was thought, would contribute to national development by being better mothers, who brought up their children as informed, useful citizens. By the 1970s, women's illiteracy rates had been cut to about 30 per cent, compared with about 25 per cent among men, the widest differences remaining in the poorest countries (Bethell 1994b: 520–8; Cubitt 1995: 113).

Initially at least, however, these developments did not give women any significant weight in the political process. Very few secured electoral office. Their voting behaviour usually seems to have closely followed that of men. The small minority of women who entered government were mainly confined to policy areas stereotyped as 'feminine': social welfare, education, health, and culture. In the populist period the only woman who took a notable public role was Juan Perón's wife Eva (Evita). During his first term as president of Argentina (1946–51) she established a remarkable mass appeal through personal charisma and her work in dispensing social benefits. Overwhelming support from newly enfranchised women voters helped Juan Perón to secure re-election under difficult circumstances in 1951. But Evita died the following year. She had always subscribed to conventional principles of female subordination, and her legacy did not prevent Perón's overthrow by a military coup in 1955. Women's role in Peronism dwindled, and the movement's subsequent strength derived, above all, from its predominantly male trade union base (Skidmore and Smith 2001: 86–9).

Rather paradoxically, women became more prominent in Latin American public life under the military dictatorships of the 1970s. Mobilization took three main forms: human rights campaigns, feminist groups (these first two largely middle class), and neighbourhood associations involving poorer women over economic or welfare demands.

The best-known women's human rights movement was begun in Argentina in 1977 by mothers seeking information about their children who had disappeared through the military regime's indiscriminate 'dirty war' against radical subversion and terrorism. The repression, which claimed at least 10,000 victims of kidnapping, torture, and secret execution, fell with greatest severity on young people. The mothers of the disappeared began holding weekly protest meetings at the Plaza de Mayo in Buenos Aires, where they attracted international publicity. The regime, committed to a traditionalist rhetoric extolling 'family values' and the role of motherhood, felt unable to act with its usual harshness against the demonstrators. The mothers of the Plaza de Mayo kept alive the question of human rights abuses and made an important contribution to the wave of popular protests that forced the military junta from office in 1983 after the Falklands debacle (Jaquette 1989: 72–8). Similar women's movements appeared as a response to repressive dictatorships elsewhere, in Chile, Uruguay, El Salvador, and Guatemala (Radcliffe and Westwood 1993: 16–19, 30–64).

Latin American feminist groups drew encouragement from the 'women's liberation' ideology which had appeared in North America and Europe during the 1960s. Diffusion of this new thinking was aided by the rapid gains which women made in higher education and consequently in middle-class, professional employment. Such opportunities were greatly enlarged by the military governments' programmes of technical modernization. For example, female enrolments at Brazil's universities increased five-fold between 1969 and 1975, while that of men only doubled; by 1980 the number of male and female students in the country's universities was roughly equal. Some individuals acquired a heightened feminist consciousness through periods of exile abroad as refugees from political persecution. The

United Nations designation of 1975 as International Women's Year, a gesture recognized by several Latin American governments, gave further prominence to the feminist cause (Jaquette 1989: 2–27).

The community groups in which women took a prominent role have already been mentioned (Chapter 5) as examples of the grass-roots NSMs seeking better welfare provision that appeared under military rule, especially in the big city shanty settlements, when political parties and trade unions were closely controlled. These institutions, concerned with national issues and the world of work, had been male dominated, but women were better able to come to the fore in demanding improved health services, schools, or water supplies, matters which related directly to child care and other ack-nowledged female domestic responsibilities. Women could arrange their household tasks to make time for attending meetings or for lobbying municipal departments during office hours. The mothers' clubs promoted by priests and nuns as part of the Catholic Church's parochial work often provided a useful organizational base.

Examples of welfare-related campaigns in which women became conspicuous include the Cost of Living Movements (protesting against inflation) and the Health Movements (to secure neighbour-hood medical centres) that appeared in São Paulo and other Brazilian cities during the later years of the military dictatorship. As a response to the 1980s economic crisis, women organized communal kitchens in many Latin American shanty town districts, with the aim of coun-teracting rising food and fuel prices by bulk purchase, and leaving more free time for paid work. The community-based welfare projects favoured by national governments and international agencies since the 1980s (Chapter 6) have particularly tried to encourage women's participation (Roberts 1995: 204–5).

It is argued that these different movements – human rights, femin-ist, and welfare – developed interconnections, so that women were radicalized and given a stronger sense of common identity through new opportunities for joint action outside their own homes. Acceptance of women's freedom to organize collectively certainly represented a major change in social attitudes. Many middle-class feminists sought to move beyond rarefied intellectual discourse by making contact with women in poorer districts. Thus, Latin American women became more generally assertive and self-confident, able to push their concerns higher up the political agenda and change aspects of their personal lives. For example, an important feminist prin-ciple is the right of women to contraception, so feminist-influenced community movements gave prominence to birth control in their discussion groups and propaganda. Women whose aspirations had been raised by political activism were persuaded of the benefits of smaller families as a way to give themselves and their children greater opportunities (Radcliffe and Westwood 1993: 88–111, 129–30, 148).

However, it is recognized also that the effectiveness of women's mobilizations has been limited in several respects. Argentina's mothers of the Plaza de Mayo, the most notable human rights activists, tried to assure the integrity and moral force of their cause by declaring themselves 'above politics'. They focused exclusively on the issue of their missing children, and would not allow the campaign to be used for broader radical or feminist aims. Yet, the mothers failed to sustain their influence after the restoration of democracy, or secure a full investigation of the disappearances. In Argentina and other Latin American countries civilian politicians, with national reconciliation as their main objective, have been concerned not to antagonize the military, and prepared to draw a veil over many of the human rights abuses committed under the dictatorships (Jaquette 1989: 72–94). When the shift back to democracy began, divisions appeared among Latin American feminists between the supporters of rival 'mainstream' male-dominated political parties. Among poorer women there is still a tendency to regard feminism as an alien, upper-class doctrine, and a feeling that politics remains 'men's business' (Jaquette 1989: 46–50). Some mothers' clubs have continued under clerical influence, stressing women's role in home making and child care. While the São Paulo Health Movement has survived, because of the ongoing concern for medical provision, the Crèche Movement, a key element in the feminist programme for emancipating women from domestic work, proved ephemeral. The economic hardship resulting from the debt crisis, and women's need to seek paid work, has left them with less time and energy for community activism (Radcliffe and Westwood 1993: 66–7, 102, 173–96). Men have sometimes moved in to take control of community organizations which have attracted official funding as a result of the shift towards decentralized welfare provision, even when the rank and file membership is mainly female.

Since the early 1980s, Latin American governments have been at pains to show their good intentions by establishing new ministries and agencies devoted to women's issues. The revision of civil codes has cut back male privileges in family law, for example regarding divorce and the custody of children. There has been a slight increase in the number of successful female electoral candidates and of women holding ministerial posts (Vanden and Prevost 2002: 109). However, on the whole the practical results from the enhancement of women's political role have been modest, as shown by the limited progress made in reforming state welfare services (Chapter 6).

Personal and family relations

A long-standing characteristic of Latin American family structure, at least among the poor, is the custom of unformalized, consensual marriages (*compromisos*). Often these unions are unstable, leading to a high proportion (about 25 per cent) of female-headed households, usually resulting from male desertions (Bethell 1994a: 23–6). The difficulties faced by such households are another factor aggravating deprivation and inequality. Many of the homeless 'street children' found in Latin American cities come from disrupted families. Family breakdown has apparently become more common in recent years (Chant 2002: 547). This aspect of Latin American life contrasts with East Asia, where kinship ties are relatively strong at all social levels.

Within this context, to what extent have domestic relations between women and men been modified? The evidence is conflicting. The greater frequency with which women have undertaken paid work may have improved their bargaining position in the family, and allowed mothers to set daughters an example of independent behaviour. Conversely, men's authority may have suffered from the post-1982 decline in their earnings, especially marked for higher-paid formal sector manual workers. Women, as a rule, spend a larger proportion of their income than do men on household and children, so perhaps increased female labour force participation has limited the harm done to welfare by the 1980s recession. Political and community activism, whether or not consciously feminist, has broken down the customary exclusion of women from the public domain, given them new sources of information, and increased their self-confidence by bringing them together for mutual support outside the home, often challenging the claims of jealous, suspicious male partners. For example, a woman who has become knowledgeable on the subject is more likely to assert her right to contraception against the objections of a husband who regards numerous children as proof of his virility.

However, women are still confined for the most part to relatively low-paid work, limiting their household budgetary contribution and its effect on the domestic balance of power. When a woman works her husband may reserve more of his own earnings for drink, cigarettes, and other personal expenditure. Some authors imply that the post-1982 economic crisis has affected women even more severely than men. Many of the better female jobs in government welfare services have fallen victim to public spending cuts; the growth of women's employment has been concentrated in street vending and other poorly rewarded informal sector occupations (Chant 2002: 549–52). Men have shown little inclination to help more at home when their wives go out to work, so Latin American women, with few of the domestic appliances that are generally available in developed countries, must carry an intensified 'double burden' of paid employment and household tasks. (Cuba's radical 1975 Family Code, requiring both marriage partners to share household duties, has not been imitated anywhere else in the region.) Part of the extra burden has fallen on daughters withdrawn from school, at the expense of their future prospects, to assist with housekeeping and the care of younger children, so that mothers can take paid work (Chant 1991: 210–12). One study, of a low-income Ecuador urban neighbourhood, reports an increase during the 1980s of domestic violence against women, caused by economic stresses in those households, still the majority, where the man remains the sole adult breadwinner (Radcliffe and Westwood 1993: 192).

Nevertheless, it must be noted that the available statistics for Latin America as a whole do not yet show any recent deterioration of female life expectancy, either in absolute terms or relative to male standards, though there has been a slight relative decline of girls' school enrolment (Table 7.1). Perhaps the effect of economic hardship in raising women's mortality has been offset by the declining birth rate and the consequently reduced likelihood of death in childbirth.

Conclusion

The status of Latin American women has improved over recent decades, a trend with various implications for the region's economic potential, some favourable, and others of more doubtful value. Contraception has become more widespread and birth rates have fallen, broadly matching trends elsewhere, though at a less rapid pace than in East Asia. Slower population growth will make it easier to achieve increases in output per head. Since the 1960s Latin American women have taken an important role in neighbourhood self-help organizations, probably securing some welfare gains and at least mitigating the social costs of the debt crisis. Women's protests against the human rights abuses perpetrated under military rule helped to discredit authoritarian government and consolidate the restored democracies. However, Latin American women's labour force participation has remained comparatively low, partly because employment protection measures have limited female recruitment by manufacturing industry. Heightened feminist consciousness entails extra pressures and demands on elected politicians, possibly interfering with the pursuit of development goals.

8 The natural environment

Relative to its population, Latin America is more generously endowed with agricultural land, forests, fresh water, and valuable mineral deposits, than any other Third World region. Nevertheless, since the 1940s the growth of population and economic activity have undoubtedly put pressure on these natural resources. This chapter first examines deforestation, the aspect of Latin American resource depletion that has recently attracted most notice. We then consider some interrelationships between economic and environmental issues. It has been argued that the 1980s debt crisis resulted, at least in part, from a wasteful use of natural resources, combined with an excessive reliance on capital-, energy- and chemical-intensive technologies. For example, farmers had become too dependent on imported fertilizers and other petroleum-based agricultural inputs. A lasting recovery can, therefore, only be achieved with development put on a 'greener', more 'sustainable', ecologically sensitive basis (Goodman and Redclift 1991; Murray 1994: 136–47). However, many observers claim that the renewed fashion for export-led growth strategies is inevitably aggravating the depletion of the natural resource base in a most dangerous way. This point has become a key part of the 'anti-globalization' case against neoliberalism. On the other hand, neoliberal advocates believe that market forces and well-designed institutions can adequately manage threats to the natural environment (Buxton and Phillips 1999a: 189–91). How far and in what ways have Latin America's recent economic problems had an environmental aspect?

Deforestation

In the early twentieth century, about 55–60 per cent of Latin America's surface area was covered by woodland, principally the tropical rainforests of Central America and the Amazon basin, where sparse indigenous populations continued in more or less complete isolation from 'mainstream' national society. European conquest and settlement had impacted only marginally on the forest zones, through slave raiding against the Amerindians and some missionary efforts. A short-lived boom in the collecting of wild rubber from Amazonia, to supply the developed countries new bicycle and automobile industries, was brought to an end just before the First World War by the establishment of lower-cost plantation production in South-east Asia.

Then various influences led to more systematic encroachment on the forests. During the 1930s, oil was discovered in the Amazon regions of several Andean countries (Colombia, Ecuador, Peru, Bolivia). The road building that followed to serve the oilfields and assert control over potentially valuable national territory also encouraged some agricultural colonization. The chemical pesticide DDT, invented in 1939, made feasible the control of endemic malaria and other diseases which previously had deterred migration from the *sierra* to the humid tropical lowlands. The Second World War and the Japanese occupation of South-east Asia caused a brief upsurge in the gathering of natural rubber, chicle (then the raw material for chewing gum), and other forest products. As population growth accelerated during the 1940s and 1950s, many Latin American politicians came to see frontier expansion as a social safety valve, a convenient way of making land available for the rural poor and relieving pressure for agrarian reform. The shift away from export dependence associated with ISI apparently required the fuller development of internal resources. This attitude was strikingly expressed by Brazil's relocation of its federal government from Rio de Janeiro 600 miles inland to the new capital city of Brasília, a project begun in 1956.

Brazil's 1964 military coup gave a further impetus to the opening up of the country's Amazon territories. The armed forces had a professional interest in securing the remote western and northern frontiers against foreign penetration. Ambitious road and airfield construction projects advertised the military's organizational competence. Exploitation of the region's natural wealth would help to establish Brazil as a leading world power. Amazonia took an important role in the new regime's plans to increase and diversify the country's exports. It was hoped that forested land could be converted to cattle ranching, a strategy supported for Brazil and other parts of Latin America by development 'experts' and international financial agencies, including the World Bank. Experiments in Australia had shown the possibilities for improving tropical pastures with introduced grass species, mainly of African origin. Modern motor trucks could haul live animals to slaughter over long distances. (Hitherto, beef production for export had been concentrated in regions such as the Argentine pampas where there were dense railway networks.) Meat consumption within Latin America was rising strongly, because of income growth. Export prospects for lower-grade beef were good, as a result of the shift of eating habits in the developed countries towards hamburgers and other fast foods.

From the mid-1960s the Brazilian government introduced a system of subsidies and fiscal incentives which particularly favoured large-scale Amazonian cattle ranching. Investment outlays could be set against tax liabilities incurred on business operations elsewhere. Corporate enterprises, many of them based in the industrial southeast, secured extensive land grants, and displaced, often violently, considerable numbers of peasant settlers who had occupied smallholdings without legal title. The squatters were pushed further westwards ahead of the capitalist ranching frontier. Settler penetration into Amazonia was helped by government road construction, and the logging trails established to extract timber (Branford and Glock 1985).

Plate 8.1 Brazil, 1972: a newly completed section of the Trans-Amazon Highway (Bettmann/Corbis)

During the early 1970s, the big business orientation of Brazilian policy was briefly supplemented by programmes for establishing small-scale farmers as colonists along the Trans-Amazon Highway (Plate 8.1) and other newly built roads, to absorb surplus population from the drought-stricken northeastern states. Planners hoped that Amazon development might, thus, stem the influx of impoverished rural migrants to the cities. However, the results from officially sponsored settlement based on small farms proved very disappointing, with many of the intended beneficiaries giving up their plots after just a few years. Such schemes failed partly through unfavourable geography. Although the rainforests' luxuriant vegetation gives an appearance of great natural fertility, in fact, soil quality is usually low. Adequate crops can be grown for two or three years on newly cleared land, after the tree cover has been felled and burnt. Then yields decline rapidly as nutrients are leached away by tropical rains, and weed infestation takes hold.

These problems might have been eased by more careful planning and management. However, the advance surveys lacked sufficient detail to identify the scattered areas of relatively fertile land, so roads and farms were laid out with little regard for long-term agricultural potential. The extension services providing the settlers with technical advice were cumbersome and understaffed. There were long delays in granting land titles and bank loans. Low construction standards made the new roads impassable for much of the rainy season, limiting farmers' ability to market their crops (Goodman and Hall 1990: 70–8). Perhaps the projects' weak performance was also due partly to the poverty and limited skills of the settlers themselves. Those coming from the northeast had usually been subsistence cultivators, sharecroppers, or landless estate labourers, with little previous experience in commercial farm management.

A rare instance of prosperous agriculture on the Brazilian rainforest frontier is Tomé-Açú, a settlement founded before the Second World War by colonists of Japanese origin. They established the cultivation of black pepper for export, the first farmers outside Asia to do so, and then moved into other specialities when the crop began to suffer from disease. Tomé-Açú's success apparently resulted from a strong capacity for cooperative action, which some observers attribute to Japanese cultural values (Goodman and Hall 1990: 366–7).

Official disillusionment with small farmer settlement reinforced the emphasis on large capitalist enterprises as the basis for opening up Brazilian Amazonia, a process that continued at an accelerating pace during the 1970s. A speculative upsurge in land prices gave an extra stimulus to the demand for ranching grants. Brazil's system of estate taxation, assessed at a lower rate on 'improved' acreage, encouraged the rapid conversion of forest to pasture. Corporate business investors, commonly absentees with little farming knowledge, applied unsuitable methods to their newly acquired properties, reducing the chances of long-term agricultural viability. Trees were cleared using heavy tractors which compacted the soil. A perceived disadvantage of more labour-intensive tree-felling with machetes and chain saws was that workers brought in for the task might seek to remain as squatters. While trying to establish pastures, developers made excessive use of chemical weedkillers, especially the compound Tordon, which included the defoliant 'Agent Orange' employed by the US for removing tree cover in Vietnam. The end of the Vietnam War made available large surplus stocks of Agent Orange during the mid-1970s. Careless herbicide applications killed the nitrogen-fixing leguminous plants required in many areas to complement introduced fodder grasses. So, while cattle ranching attracted considerable investments and destroyed extensive rainforest tracts, its productivity was very low (Branford and Glock 1985: 43–81).

Some land grants were developed by private sector colonization companies, drawing family farmers who had been displaced from coffee growing in southeastern Brazil by the extension of soya beans and other highly mechanized crops. Such enterprises enjoyed rather more success than government schemes, through better management and the selection of relatively prosperous colonists. However, most small farmer settlement was spontaneous, individual, and unplanned. From the late 1970s, as the 'Brazilian miracle' of rapid economic growth faded, industrial recession took hold, and chances of finding work in eastern cities diminished, more of the rural migrant poor sought a livelihood on the Amazon frontier. The attempts of some provincial governors to check colonization became increasingly ineffective as *abertura* weakened the military regime. Surface gold strikes attracted numerous small-scale prospectors and diggers, known as *garimpeiros*. Mining development also occurred on a large-scale capitalist basis, most notably through the undertaking formed to exploit the Carajás iron ore deposits, discovered in 1967. By the mid-1980s the Greater Carajás complex extended over 300,000 square miles, an area as big as Britain and France. It included mines, hydroelectric dams, a 550-mile railway, and associated agricultural colonies. Pig-iron smelters were planned, posing a further threat to the forest through the demand for charcoal as fuel. At the same time improved satellite imagery became available to map changes in land use, indicating how Amazon tree cover was being lost through felling and burning at an accelerating rate, and suggesting that much of the region would be entirely deforested within a few years. The subject attracted widespread media attention in the developed countries. Amazon deforestation, it was argued, would release large quantities of carbon into the atmosphere, and contribute to the recently identified phenomenon of global warming through the 'greenhouse effect' (Branford and Glock 1985: 84–90, 156–8; Goodman and Hall 1990: 136–41, 385–7). There was concern, too, over the threatened loss of potentially valuable biological species.

The causes of Central American deforestation were broadly similar to those at work in Amazonia, with some distinctive features. From the 1950s, there was extensive clearance of forested lowland areas to grow cotton for export, supplementing coffee and bananas, the region's established staples. Commercial cotton production had been made feasible here by the introduction of DDT. The expansion of cattle ranching followed in the 1960s, strongly influenced by the 'hamburger connection' with the US, while traditional *haciendas* began evicting many of their labour tenants as a response to agrarian reform proposals and minimum wage laws. The replacement of ox-draught ploughing with tractors made it possible to conduct agricultural operations with a reduced workforce. Guatemala's military rulers, especially brutal and grasping, enriched themselves through the acquisition of large tracts in the Peten forest region when its oil-bearing potential became clear (Rouquié 1987: 297). Because Central America's industrialization and urbanization were more limited than Brazil's, a larger proportion of the landless poor sought to become established as frontier settlers. Conflict between squatters and encroaching estates developed into widespread guerrilla movements by the 1970s. Much of the road building that accompanied frontier expansion was financed with US aid, provided with an eye to counter-insurgency needs.

Environmental conditions and the debt crisis: problems of 'sustainability'?

To what extent have environmental problems been responsible for Latin America's debt crisis of the early 1980s, and the region's subsequent difficulties in achieving a sustained economic recovery? Points made by authors who stress ecological aspects include the wastefulness and the incidental costs of deforestation. Land exposed by the removal of tree cover is subject to rapid erosion. Topsoil loss has been most severe in the Andean countries and Central America, where estate enlargement and the pressure of rural population growth have pushed peasant cultivators up steep mountain slopes. As well as degrading the newly cleared land, hill wash causes silt to accumulate in reservoirs, reducing the capacity of hydroelectric and irrigation facilities. Also, because forest canopy holds moisture and contributes to rainfall by releasing water vapour, deforestation increases the likelihood of drought. For example, Ecuador takes 60 per cent of its electricity supplies from a single hydroelectric scheme. In 1995, the country suffered its worst power cuts for 30 years, through drought combined with sedimentation. In Panama, where the share of land under forest has declined from 70 per cent to 30 per cent since 1945, lower rainfall threatens the viability of the trans-isthmian canal, a crucial revenue source (Green 1991: 37–43).

Another topic attracting notice is the damage caused by pesticides. This problem became most conspicuous in Central America, where the post-1945 extension of cotton cultivation over the coastal plains depended on DDT applications against boll weevil and malarial mosquitoes. Technical support came from North American chemical companies, and agricultural supply firms based in the southern US cotton growing states. Central American conditions – geographically concentrated monocropping, high humidity, and the absence of winter frosts (unlike the US south) – made pest control especially difficult. Therefore, growers responded with heavier pesticide usage, insect strains quickly built up resistance, and applications had to be repeated ever more frequently, as often as 40 or 50 times a year. On this 'pesticide treadmill' chemical inputs accounted for more than a third of cotton production costs in Guatemala, El Salvador, and Nicaragua by the late 1970s. Indiscriminate aerial spraying made pesticide poisoning a serious public health problem. Breast milk samples from women in Central American cotton growing districts show some of the highest levels of DDT ever recorded in human populations (World Bank 1992: 140). Soil erosion from deforested land combined with pesticide runoff to degrade waterways, mangrove swamps, and coastal fisheries. Central American cotton growing, itself, became uneconomic in the early 1980s, when crop prices fell, and devaluations raised the cost of imported chemicals. The region's cotton exports have subsequently dwindled to insignificance (Murray 1994).

Mexico City provides the most striking case within Latin America of urban environmental problems. The city lies at an altitude of 6,000–7,000 feet on Mexico's central plateau, in a valley basin encircled by mountains. This site, the focal point of the pre-conquest Aztec empire, was taken by the Spanish in the sixteenth century for a colonial capital, to secure control over the subjugated Indians. Under ISI the Mexico City region came, by the 1980s, to account for about a quarter of the country's population, and nearly half of its income, industrial output, and automobile ownership. This represents the common Latin American pattern, with twentieth-century urbanization markedly concentrated in a single 'primate' city, usually the nation's capital. Mexico City's inhabitants now number more than 20 million. Urban growth on such a scale, in such a location, has generated severe atmospheric pollution from industrial plant and motor vehicles, their engine efficiency impaired by the high altitude. Dust blown from deforested hillsides is added to the smoke and exhaust fumes. Temperature inversions often trap the contaminated air within the valley basin. Apart from the human suffering and economic burden caused by the growing incidence of lung disease, corrective measures attempted since the debt crisis have required the closure of many factories (Gilbert 1994: 120). Subsidence resulting from the extraction of underground water reserves aggravated the damage caused by the 1985 earthquake. The cost of meeting the city's water demands is rising sharply, because of the need to pump in additional supplies over long distances, across mountain terrain.

The Chilean capital Santiago, with a similar mountain valley geography, has also experienced chronic air pollution, made worse by an ill-judged neoliberal deregulation of bus transport implemented under the Pinochet dictatorship. The reform caused underused services to proliferate, employing large numbers of aged, second-hand imported vehicles (Collins and Lear 1995: 231–42).

However, although these instances of economic loss through ecological damage may have local significance, the extent to which they represent a more general Latin American environmental crisis is doubtful. The pesticide-related collapse of cotton growing which occurred during the 1980s was peculiar to Central America. Cotton output held steady in South America, while over Latin America as a whole the production of bananas, another crop that involves heavy pesticide applications, rose strongly (FAO 1995: 166, 182). Since the debt crisis, several Caribbean basin countries have tried to improve their foreign trade position by growing 'non-traditional' fruit and vegetables (melons, pineapples, strawberries, broccoli, etc.) for sale to the developed world. Fruit exports have made an important contribution to Chile's economic recovery. It has been argued that because these new lines also depend on chemical pest control, they will give rise to the same environmental and public health difficulties as did cotton (Murray 1994: 56–97). However, importing countries subject horticultural products, items for human consumption, to strict quality controls. Shipments found with high chemical residue levels are excluded, obliging growers to exercise more restraint in their use of pesticides.

The recent record on urban air quality is mixed rather than wholly unfavourable. In Mexico City and Santiago pollution has been reduced since the early 1990s, partly through stricter controls on motor vehicle emissions. However, in Brazil's São Paulo conurbation, the most important Latin American manufacturing zone, air pollution fell during the early 1980s but subsequently held steady, with progress against industrial emissions being offset by the massive growth of vehicle numbers (Baer 2001: 389–95, 414; *The Economist* 2002). In the developed countries, public concern aroused during the 1960s over environmental standards led to the tighter regulation of emission levels, and new technologies for pollution control. These technologies have since become more widely available, to make possible the improvement of conditions in 'middle income' Latin America. The worst urban air pollution now occurs in 'low-income' countries, such as India and China (World Bank 1992: 50–3, 199; World Bank 2001b: 174–5). During the last two decades, Latin American urban growth has slackened, and become more widely dispersed over a range of provincial towns, rather than being concentrated in a few unwieldy primate cities (Roberts 1995: 90–1, 208). These changes result partly from the turn away from state-led ISI.

Care must also be taken to avoid sweeping generalizations on the subject of forest clearance. The process has certainly been very rapid in Central America, reducing the wooded area at an annual rate of 2 or 3 per cent, and causing considerable incidental damage (World Bank 1996: 206–7). Population densities here are quite high, so land hunger among the rural poor and the need for increased agricultural exports to service foreign debt have kept up the momentum of deforestation (Goodman and Redclift 1991: 184–204). However, in Brazilian Amazonia, which accounts for more than half of Latin America's forested area, the situation now seems to be rather less ominous than was once supposed. During the mid-1980s published assessments indicated that about 23,200 square miles of rainforest were being lost each year, a 1.8 per cent annual depletion rate (Goodman and Hall 1990: 386). Estimates of the annual loss were subsequently revised downwards to 8,100 square miles (0.6 per cent) for the 1978–88 period, and during the later 1980s the clearance rate fell, reaching 5,300 square miles (0.4 per cent) in 1990, though it rose again to about 7,000 square miles (0.5 per cent) in the later 1990s (World Bank 1993: 323; Baer 2001: 408).

There are several reasons why the pace of Brazilian deforestation eased. When criticism of the 'assault on the Amazon' first began to appear in the developed world, reactions from Brazil were predominantly hostile. Environmentalism was represented, especially by the military, landowners, and big business, as an 'imperialist' First World doctrine, propagated with the aim of shackling the country's development. However, groups under threat from development projects – rubber tappers, small farmers, *garimpeiros*, forest Indians – had been evolving organized forms of collective resistance and self-defence during the later years of military rule. Amazon grassroots mobilizations of the NSM type gained extra strength by establishing contact with foreign conservationist NGOs. For example, in 1987 Chico Mendes, a rubber tappers' leader, drew attention to their cause on a highly successful visit to the US. The following year he was murdered at the instigation of landowners opposed to his campaign for establishing a forest reserve. This much-publicized killing caused outrage both within Brazil and abroad (Goodman and Redclift 1991: 117–18; Green 1991: 41–2). Many Indian peoples also drew encouragement from NGO activists and the end of authoritarian rule to mount impressive campaigns in defence of their traditional lands (Cubitt 1995: 70–9). The environmentalist cause gained support from a broader range of Brazilian anti-elite opinion and became a significant force in national politics. Official conservation measures were strengthened as a result.

Lobbying by US environmentalists concerned about global warming, an issue given extra prominence by the drought that affected North America in 1988, obliged the World Bank to cut funding for projects, such as dam building and road asphalting, that might encourage deforestation. Political circumstances and financial constraints forced the Brazilian government to end its subsidies for the establishment of new cattle ranches. Some progress has been made through research and experiment on methods of upgrading older, low quality pastures, as an alternative to further land clearance (National Research Council 1993: 316–18). From the later 1980s, migration into Amazonia by poor settlers and fortune seekers also declined. The federal government no longer had the resources for initiating major new highway construction schemes. Inadequate maintenance allowed many stretches of the trunk roads built during the 1960s and 1970s to become impassable and overgrown. A modest revival of industrial activity improved employment prospects elsewhere. Gold strikes became less frequent; most of the surface deposits accessible to *garimpeiros* are now probably exhausted.

Nevertheless, powerful forces are still at work encroaching on the forest. While the capacity of the federal government for promoting development has been curtailed, Brazil's new constitution, enacted in 1988, gives individual states greater autonomy and a larger share of tax revenues. Territories formerly under federal administration have been granted statehood for the first time. Amazon state governors are anxious to please their constituents, for example by building feeder roads that open up new areas for settlement. Immigration has declined, but local population growth through natural increase continues. An increase of selective logging for export, largely instigated by companies from South-east Asia, where timber reserves are already depleted (Baer 2001: 408), is making extensive tracts of natural forest more vulnerable to desiccation and fire damage. There has been no significant agrarian reform to reduce inequalities in landownership. Much of the growth in cattle ranching involves smaller herds, whose owners never received subsidies and are not affected by the loss of public support. Because credit is now scarce and expensive, ranchers upgrading their pastures commonly dispose of their remaining timber reserves to obtain finance. Very little has been done to establish more sustainable agricultural practices among small settlers, by technical assistance and the granting of secure property titles. During the 1980s underfunding and greater politicization impaired the effectiveness of research institutions concerned with agricultural development in Amazonia (National Research Council 1993: 309, 318–42). An implicit subsidy for extensive development remains through the practice of *Petrobrás*, the federal governments' monopoly petroleum enterprise, in maintaining uniform motor vehicle fuel prices throughout Brazil, without regard to transport costs.

So, land clearance continues. On current trends about a fifth of the Amazonian rainforest will have been destroyed by 2010 and about 40 per cent by the middle of the century. This may accelerate global warming and deprive humanity of valuable biological species. It will certainly threaten many of the surviving indigeneous forest peoples. However, environmental change, even if undesirable in itself, is not yet a major constraint on the Brazilian economy as a whole. Indeed, some recent studies now suggest that Amazonian settlement has, so far, on balance, been a cost-effective enterprise, with useful economic results. This is suggested by the way land clearance revived during the 1990s, despite the withdrawal of government subsidies and fiscal incentives. Income per head and welfare standards have risen more rapidly in Brazil's western frontier states than across the rest of the country. In the *cerrado*, part of the 'Legal Amazonia' administrative region, though natural savanna lying outside the rainforest area, there has been a remarkable growth of soya bean, beef, and cotton production. The *cerrado* export-oriented agricultural boom, based on public sector crop research to cope with soil acidity, covers a vast territory and shows no sign of being checked by environmental depletion (Andersen *et al.* 2002). There may be a similar development potential in most of Brazil's South American neighbours, where natural resources remain abundant, except for the densely populated highland regions of Bolivia, Peru, and Ecuador. Forests still cover about 47 per cent of Latin America's land area: 63 per cent in Brazil, 48 per cent in South America as a whole, but only 31 per cent in Mexico and Central America (World Bank 2001b: 138–40). It has been suggested that natural resource constraints are limiting Chile's 'non-traditional' commodity exports (Buxton and Phillips 1999a: 191), but there is little evidence to support this view. Chilean agriculture remains comparatively resilient. The country's late 1990s economic slowdown came, above all, from the falling price of copper, together with declines in manufacturing, investment, and construction (ECLAC 2002: 128).

To what extent can grassroots mobilization provide a defence against pressures on the environment? Popular movements have helped to check some large-scale Amazonian development projects, and thus slow down the rate of deforestation since the mid-1980s. Nevertheless, it is doubtful whether joint action by the poor will be able to play a more positive, constructive role over the longer term. 'Social forestry' initiatives, making local communities responsible for woodland management, have shown some promise as a conservation strategy in South and East Asia, where there are long traditions of stable peasant village life. However, in Latin America group ties and identities among rural people are relatively weak, after several centuries of estate domination. Since the 1980s, public sector agencies and NGOs have encouraged collective action by frontier colonists, but with limited results (Hall 1997: 187–8, 198–9). Successful cooperation among rainforest settlers to solve technical problems and achieve agricultural sustainability, exemplified by the Japanese farmers of Tomé-Açú, remains rare.

Conclusion

Latin American deforestation accelerated between the 1930s and the 1970s, as a result of population growth and new economic opportunities. By the 1980s the loss of forest cover was causing widespread alarm. Other notable environmental issues include the overuse of agricultural pesticides and urban air pollution. However, Latin America's natural resources are relatively abundant, so ecological degradation has probably not been a major cause of the region's recent economic difficulties, except in Central America and parts of the Andean highlands. Yet, whatever the facts of the case, perceptions of an acute and growing Latin American ecological crisis have certainly taken hold in the developed countries, especially the US, with significant policy results. Environmental concerns were raised by US opponents of NAFTA, and nearly blocked it. The issue persists as an obstacle to further commercial liberalization through the FTAA project (Smith 1996: 251–62).

9 Latin America in the twenty-first century

Problems and potential

What has neoliberalism achieved in Latin America? What are the region's current prospects after some two decades on the new policy line? It is, of course, impossible to predict with any confidence, especially bearing in mind the local record of instability and unexpected misfortune. Table 9.1 presents various statistics of recent Latin American economic performance, distinguishing four main phases. The first of these phases (1975–81) saw considerable economic growth and large-scale capital inflows. Then the 1982 debt crisis sharply curtailed external funding and interest payments rose, bringing a substantial resource transfer out of the region (Table 9.1, column 6). Output per head and export earnings declined. Resource inflows and economic growth resumed in the early 1990s, but another reversal followed towards the end of the decade when international trade and finance once again lost their buoyancy. Statists can, therefore, claim that free market reform has accomplished little; Latin America still seems caught in a cycle of economic failure, cruelly vulnerable to outside forces. From the neoliberal point of view, on the other hand, it may be possible to detect some underlying changes which give hope for the future.

The 1991–7 output per head growth phase differs from that of the 1975–81 period in being achieved with a lower investment rate (Table 9.1, column 7). This was possible partly because the rate of population increase had fallen, but also suggests some improvement in efficiency. Furthermore, the post-1998 recession is, so far, concentrated on Argentina and Venezuela; across the region at large, economic slowdown has been less abrupt, widespread, and severe than in the 1980s (Table 2.1). The difference, to some extent, reflects the international context. Since 1998 world trade growth has continued, though at a reduced pace, unlike the sharp decrease of the early 1980s. However, Latin American exports are now also more

Table 9.1 Economic trends in Latin America, 1975–2002

| | | | | Share of GDP (%) | | | | |
	(1)	(2)	(3)	(4)	(5)	(6)*	(7)	(8)
1975–81	1.8	5.9	58.7	3.9	1.8	+2.1	24	22
1982–90	−0.6	−1.7	21.0	1.3	4.1	−2.8	18	21
1991–97	1.8	7.1	55.1	3.9	2.6	+1.3	20	19
1998–2002	−0.1	2.1	65.6	4.2	3.4	+0.8	20	19

Sources: Estimated from Bethell 1994a: 228, 241, 245; IMF 1996; World Bank 1990–2003; World Bank 2002b; ECLAC 2002.

Note: *Column (6) is roughly equivalent to column (4) minus (5) and to (7) minus (8).

Key to columns: (1) Annual growth of output per head (%); (2) Annual growth of exports (%); (3) Annual net capital inflows (billion 1990 US $s). Share of GDP (%): (4) Net capital inflows; (5) Payments abroad of interest and profits; (6) Resource transfer to (+) or from (−) the region; (7) Regional investment rate; (8) Regional savings rate.

diversified, and better able to contend with an adverse trading climate, increasing their market share, a contrast with the 1980s experience (Table 9.1, column 2). The recent decline of inward resource transfers has occurred gradually (Table 9.1, column 6), because DFI became more important than relatively volatile bank lending and portfolio finance, and because developed country interest rates have been falling. On the whole, Latin American price inflation and foreign debt charges remain low by previous standards (Tables 2.4, 2.5). So, there are some grounds for optimism.

Nevertheless, Latin America is still beset by many problems, which make the limited development gains achieved over the last few years highly insecure. Prospects for the world economy are doubtful. While the current international trade slowdown is quite moderate compared with the early 1980s, it may prove persistent. When the 1982 debt crisis broke, the US was in recession, but with sound national finances and poised for a vigorous recovery. Demand from the US provided the main driving force behind the subsequent world export boom that ran almost continuously until the turn of the century, by which point the country had built up very large current account deficits and foreign debt. Correcting these imbalances may, sooner or later, require the US to undertake austerity measures, with a severe impact on its trading partners. Furthermore, economic liberalization and an enormous low-cost workforce have made China a highly competitive source of basic manufactured goods, limiting Latin America's ability to follow the NIC development path through labour-intensive export-led industrialization. Natural resource abundance, not yet lost by environmental degradation (Chapter 8), still gives some republics scope for increasing the output of raw materials, but commodities lack manufacturing's dynamic potential.

As with foreign trade, the current deceleration of capital inflows to Latin America is happening more slowly than that of the early 1980s but, perhaps, will be sustained longer. Privatization opportunities, the main method of recruiting DFI, are now almost exhausted. Divestiture has become highly contentious; in any case, few attractive SOEs remain unsold. Investment will have to depend more on a strengthened domestic savings effort, and there seems little likelihood of this being achieved. Latin America's savings rate was declining even during the 1991–7 prosperity phase, because of rapid increases in household consumption and in government social spending (Table 9.1, column 8; Chapters 3 and 6). Such increases may have been necessary to sugar the pill of neoliberal reform, but they checked the region's longer-term economic momentum. The outlook, at best, is thus for very slow income per head gains. Most probably, Latin America can never match the vigour of the high-saving East Asian economies.

If the free market course is yielding such limited benefits, what are the likely political implications? Popular resentment has already brought acute crises in Argentina and Venezuela. Do these episodes set the pattern for the future, or will they prove special cases, the result of particular local circumstances (Chapters 3 and 5)? Social tensions may be manageable. However mediocre the results from neoliberalism, Latin Americans, on the whole, show little sign of going back to statist alternatives. Memories of the chronic inflation associated with ISI remain. Castro's regime on Cuba, drab, stale, and oppressive, does not advertise socialism in an appealing way. Recent surveys of Latin American public opinion indicate continuing majority support for centre-right views and democracy. Attitudes towards the US are favourable on balance, though negative judgements have increased sharply since 2000. While privatization now attracts widespread hostility, most of those questioned still believe that the market economy is the only way to achieve development (*The Economist* 2003c). According to some observers, religious trends may have reinforced the neoliberal cause. Over the last 30 years there has been a striking growth of Protestantism within Latin America, eroding the historical ascendancy of the Roman Catholic Church, and appealing especially to the underprivileged. The estimated number of Latin American Protestants stood at five million in 1970 and 40 million in 1990, their share of the region's population rising from 2 per cent to 10 per cent. As the commitment of most Catholics is relatively weak, they may soon be outnumbered by Protestants among Latin America's regular church goers. The general tone of many Protestant churches is conservative, emphasizing 'other worldly' spiritual values combined with personal betterment through self-help and self-discipline (Green 1991: 132–6, 171–84; Vanden and Prevost 2002: 138–40). This contrasts with the social-reformist approach of Roman Catholic Liberation Theology, itself a declining influence since the 1970s, and may be seen as 'a powerful force of regression back to passivity' (Cubitt 1995: 88). However, diminished popular expectations from government perhaps ensure greater popular forbearance.

On the other hand, disillusionment or disgust with politicians of every stripe is also being expressed through falling election turn-outs and the loss of support by hitherto dominant parties, such as the PRI in Mexico and the Peronist PJ in Argentina. Nearly all Latin American presidents now lack a congressional majority and depend on multi-party alliances to legislate, a serious restraint on decisive action. The first stages of neoliberal reform, undertaken during the 1980s and 1990s, were in certain respects quite straightforward. The key elements – cutting protective tariff duties, curbing government expenditure, restricting the money supply to bring down inflation, beginning the privatization of state enterprises – are technically simple. They could often be implemented as executive decisions by national presidents, ministers of finance, and central bank governors. However, the necessary reinforcing measures are much more difficult to implement and, by their nature, can only bear fruit over the long term. Many entail complex new laws which must be pushed through elected assemblies, in the face of entrenched vested interests. Legislation must be drafted and administered by competent bureaucracies. Additional 'microeconomic' reforms include broadening the tax base to take a larger share of upper-class wealth, civil service recruitment more on the basis of merit rather than political clientage, the better regulation of privatized utilities, and measures for raising educational standards. Effort on all these points is required to make Latin American capitalism function successfully.

Appendix 1
Biographies

These four political biographies illustrate some of the general issues discussed in the main text.

Fernando Henrique Cardoso (1931–)

Brazilian sociologist and statesman: the most impressive national leader to have emerged in Latin America since the debt crisis, and a very unusual case of a research scholar going on to make a mark in high elected office. From an upper-middle-class military family, Cardoso embarked, in the 1950s, on a career as an academic sociologist sympathetic to Marxism, soon establishing a reputation for intellectual brilliance. Because of his well-known left-wing views, he had to flee Brazil after the 1964 military coup. Cardoso then worked for a time at the ECLA in Santiago, Chile, where he co-authored a sophisticated and discriminating contribution to dependency theory. In 1969 he returned to Brazil and secured a full professorship at the University of São Paulo, but was soon compulsorily retired, with a generous pension, when the military regime began a new phase of intensified repression. His social origins and international academic fame protected him from serious maltreatment, though while briefly held by the police he was allowed to catch sight of a less eminent detainee undergoing torture. Cardoso set up a social research institute with other displaced university colleagues and took an active role in the PMDB, the umbrella opposition party tolerated by the authorities, entering Congress as senator for the state of São Paulo. After the return to civilian government he gained further prominence through his role in drafting the 1988 democratic constitution. He became Foreign Minister in 1992 and Finance Minister in 1993, charged with tackling Brazil's chronic inflation. The success of his *real* plan for price stabilization assured him victory by a wide margin at the 1994 presidential election, with a mandate for further neoliberal measures.

However, the 1988 constitution severely limited the president's executive powers and, unlike some other economic reformers, for example Argentina's Carlos Menem (see below), Cardoso did not begin with a strong congressional base. His own party, the centre-left PSDB, recently created by secession from the PMDB, was relatively small, so he had to cooperate with various right-wing parties, each little more than groupings of regional bosses, ill-disciplined, opportunistic, and hungry for spoils. The reform effort focused on privatization and on curbing the deficit-ridden public sector pension system. The constraints of coalition government held back progress, and Brazil came close to financial collapse once again in the late 1990s, though the crisis was contained. Cardoso gave essential leadership over two presidential terms (1995–8, 1999–2002). Urbane, affable, self-assured but not arrogant, a consummate negotiator, he had established good personal relations with many key figures in Brazil's political elite during his time as a senator. He was able to manage his congressional alliances while sustaining an image of competence and integrity. He did not attempt a charismatic mass appeal and commanded respect rather than excitement or enthusiasm among the wider public. A passionate democrat, above all, his style was that of a serious-minded educator seeking to persuade by rational argument, urging the case for fiscal discipline and fuller engagement in the world economy. Cardoso also remained committed to achieving greater social justice, though he had long ago outgrown his youthful Marxism. He disliked gesture politics and did not favour the personally directed relief schemes used by some other neoliberal presidents to advertise a concern for welfare issues. Instead, he put able colleagues in charge of the social ministries (education, health, etc.) and backed up measures to improve targeting and raise organizational standards. By the end of his second term, quite modest budget increases were bringing some welfare gains. Cardoso set an example for his successor as president, Lula da Silva, who seems to be following a similar strategy of consensus building, cross-party compromise, prudent finance, and incremental social advance (Goertzel 1999; Manzetti 1999; Panizza 2000).

Fidel Castro (Ruz) (1926–)

Cuban revolutionary and dictator. The son of a wealthy self-made Spanish immigrant landowner, Castro entered the violent world of

Cuban politics as a university student during the late 1940s. He led an abortive attempt to overthrow the Batista dictatorship by attacking the Moncada army barracks (26 July 1953), was briefly imprisoned (1953–5), and left for Mexico. He returned to Cuba with a few companions in 1956 and launched a rural guerrilla campaign. After the collapse of his regime, Batista fled the island on 31 December 1958. Various other groups, quite distinct from Castro's 26th of July Movement, including a Cuban communist party, had gone into opposition and helped bring about Batista's downfall, but Castro's charisma and command of an armed following made him the Revolution's dominant figure. He seized power in 1959, at the age of only 32.

He began by proclaiming a 'humanist' ideology, neither communist nor capitalist. While large landed estates would be broken up, the exploitative presence of 'imperialist' foreign business brought to an end, and working people secured a decent livelihood, the patriotic middle classes and native entrepreneurs were seemingly to have a part in building the new Cuba. Yet, the wholesale expropriation of nationally owned firms began in 1960. In 1961, Castro declared himself a Marxist-Leninist and the Revolution socialist, inseparably allied to the Soviet Union. These moves followed a series of hostile US acts, culminating with Washington's support for the unsuccessful Bay of Pigs invasion by anti-Castro Cuban exiles (1961). Soon afterwards he defined his leadership in terms of control through a remodelled communist party, and has maintained this position ever since, with various adjustments on points of detail. The Castro regime weathered the 1989–91 collapse of the Soviet Union and its Eastern European empire, despite the devastating loss of Soviet trade subsidies, and unlike other surviving communist dictatorships (China, Vietnam) has not pursued comprehensive economic reform. Castro is now, by a very wide margin, the world's longest serving political leader.

Castro's durability comes partly from physical vigour (he was an outstanding school athlete), and from his relative youth when he triumphed in 1959. His key role in overthrowing a hated dictator, his successful defiance of the US, his oratorical skills, and the welfare gains he brought to poorer Cubans, won him an enormous popular appeal, a little of which still remains. Dissent has been managed through the emigration safety valve, together with an elaborate apparatus of surveillance and repression. Just why Castro's rule became so inflexibly socialist is more debatable. Almost certainly, by 1959 he had already concluded from the record of US business imperialism on Cuba that only an uncompromising anti-capitalist stance could secure national independence, though at first his full purpose was concealed for tactical reasons. But, perhaps, Washington's implacable enmity to the Revolution radicalized him further, or at least helped him push the new regime leftward (Szulc 1987; Wiarda and Kline 2000: 416–21). Similar doubts arise with more recent events. For example, in February 1996 Castro authorized the shooting down, most likely in international air space, of two unarmed civilian planes being flown on a propaganda mission by Florida-based Cuban exiles. The planes' destruction caused the US Congress to tighten economic sanctions against Cuba through the Helms-Burton Act. Had Castro been angered beyond endurance by earlier incursions? Did he feel threatened by Washington's 'reflex hostility' (Morley and McGillion 2002: 94–7)? Or was the shootdown calculated to provoke another US backlash, renew Cuba's siege mentality, and give him an excuse for curbing the half-hearted market reforms begun three years earlier in response to the loss of Soviet aid? He had been expressing distaste for this 'bourgeois' course (LeoGrande 1997: 211–12). Such questions may never be adequately answered. Though voluble and gregarious, Castro is something of an enigma, apparently now without close confidants, not given to discussing his plans or elucidating his motives.

Carlos Saúl Menem (1930–)

Argentine politician: an amoral exponent of economic liberalization 'by surprise'. The son of Syrian immigrants, Menem became a political star as a critic of the 1976–83 military dictatorship and as the flamboyant, free-spending Peronist or Justicialist Party (PJ) governor of La Rioja, a poor province in the Argentine interior. He won the 1989 presidential election for the PJ on a populist platform, but immediately after taking office began a comprehensive neoliberal adjustment programme. Non-Peronist businessmen were given important ministerial posts. Menem claimed that his spectacular policy switch was forced on him by suddenly escalating inflation and social disorder. However, it is now clear that well before he became president his associates had contacted corporate leaders, offering a pro-business line in return for campaign contributions. Menem seems to have hoped that corporate funds and election success would let him win full control over Peronism, eclipsing the movement's traditional base, the unionized working class of Buenos Aires. Politically well-connected business groups were conspicuous beneficiaries of a rapid post-1989 privatization drive. An aura of corrupt dealing hung about Menem's administration. During his first presidency (1989–95) he could employ autocratic, high-handed methods, helped by the PJ's strong position in Congress, and made extensive use of emergency decree powers. He added several compliant judges to the Supreme Court. Yet, economic recovery, apparently the effect of bold, decisive leadership, ensured his re-election for a second term (1995–9). Menem projected himself as hard-living and *macho*, keen on football, boxing, fast cars, and glamorous women. His first marriage ended in a very public and acrimonious divorce (1990). He would later remarry, at the age of 71, to a former beauty queen 35 years his junior.

Menem's popular standing underwent a rapid decline soon into his second presidency, because of the economic recession and high unemployment that followed the tequila crisis. Sharp practice and a vulgar, raffish charm lost their appeal when no longer associated with prosperity. Disillusionment was greatest among the industrial and public sector workers who had borne the main burden of restructuring. Menem tried to secure a third term in office by relaxing fiscal discipline, but Eduardo Duhalde, representing the labour wing of the PJ, was chosen as the party's presidential candidate instead. Duhalde lost the 1999 election, partly, he and his associates believed, because Menem gave him only grudging support, so tensions within Peronism were aggravated. A legacy of public sector deficits and debt destroyed the new Alliance administration in December 2001 (Chapter 3). Duhalde now became interim president, but Menem kept a capacity for mischief, encouraging his cronies on the Supreme Court to block stabilization measures, and running against two other Peronists in the 2003 presidential election. The party was now hopelessly split. Menem headed the first-round poll, though with only 24 per cent of the vote. (He had got a 48 per cent share in 1995.) Opinion surveys gave him no chance of success in the runoff, such was his unpopularity beyond a core following, so he withdrew from the contest. The second-place candidate, a rival Peronist, became president by default without full democratic legitimacy, further degrading Argentina's institutions (Manzetti 1999; Panizza 2000; Stokes 2001).

Juan Domingo Perón (1895–1974)

Argentine army officer and politician: the most famous Latin American populist leader. Of lower-middle-class parentage, Perón was commissioned from the Military Academy in 1913 and had reached the rank of colonel by 1943 when he took part in an army coup that overthrew Argentina's conservative landowner-dominated government. He was a member of an authoritarian, ultra-nationalist officer group, attracted by European fascism, and opposed to US attempts at involving Argentina, along with the rest of Latin America, in the Second World War against the Axis powers. Argentine independence, the officers believed, required neutrality in the world conflict, strict social discipline, and the build-up of national armaments production to counter the threat from Brazil, now being supplied with military equipment by Washington. Perón became the junta's Labour Minister and used the post to cultivate a popular following, arbitrating strikes in the workers' favour. He won the 1946 presidential election with overwhelming lower-class support and some middle-class votes, denouncing Argentina's landed 'oligarchy' and the developed countries' 'imperialism'. US criticism of him as a fascist misfired badly. He offered social harmony through a 'Justicialist' third way between capitalism and communism. The military were promised the vigorous development of strategic industries.

During the first years of Perón's presidency, national income was redistributed on a massive scale to urban labour, a shift made possible by the post-war commodity boom. Argentina's agricultural exports (mainly beef and wheat) were taxed to hold down domestic food prices, fund ISI, and enlarge state sector employment. The British-owned railways and many other utilities were nationalized. Perón's popular appeal came, in part, from his second wife, the actress María Eva Duarte ('Evita'), a strident peroxide blonde, of humble origins and with the common touch. (His first wife, a school teacher, had died in 1938.) Evita gave him support with charismatic oratory and the work of her semi-official charitable foundation. She helped assure his re-election to a second presidential term in 1951, even though by this time ISI exhaustion had brought economic growth to a halt. Perón's regime combined democratic forms with increasingly authoritarian methods: a pervasive leadership cult, state control over the media, and the intimidation of opponents. The Peronist movement had a thuggish, street-fighting aspect, echoing European fascism. These and other distasteful features were accentuated after Evita's death from cancer (1952). Perón showed an unseemly enthusiasm for teenage schoolgirls, and became embroiled in conflict with the Catholic Church, provoking his overthrow by a military coup (1955). He was exiled and eventually settled in Madrid.

Following Perón's removal, a succession of military and civilian governments tried to revive Argentine economic development. These efforts entailed austerity at the expense of labour and met fierce trade union resistance, sustained by memories of the mid-1940s golden age. From exile, Perón encouraged his followers' intransigence, and when a more moderate collaborationist union leadership began emerging, gave tacit support to a new generation of young ultra-left radicals who had embarked on revolutionary struggle. Left-wing armed action and the right-wing backlash threatened Argentina with chaos. So the military let Perón return, at the age of 78, in failing health, and win election to the presidency once again (1973). Only he seemed capable of restoring order. As vice-presidential running mate, Perón chose his third wife, an ex-night club dancer, of limited intelligence and clearly unfit for a senior government post. He died in 1974. His widow then held the presidency through a disastrous interlude of mounting social conflict until 1976, when another military dictatorship took charge. Yet, a widely supported Peronist (Justicialist) party survived.

Behind a genial, engaging manner, Perón was cold, cynical and unprincipled, with little affection for the working people whose cause he espoused. Lacking physical courage himself, he sanctioned violence by others to suit his purpose. It was, perhaps, inevitable that Argentina's ISI would be particularly contentious, because basic foodstuffs were the trade staple, putting the export elite directly at odds with a large urban proletariat. However, Perón accentuated the country's political polarization and economic disappointment (Page 1983; Wiarda and Kline 2000: 108–17; Vanden and Prevost 2002: 403–30).

Appendix 2
Chronology

1492	Christopher Columbus reaches the Caribbean.
1500	Portuguese sailors reach Brazil.
1810–25	All the mainland Latin American colonies gain independence.
1823	US President James Monroe's declaration against any further attempts by European powers to extend their political presence in the Americas (the 'Monroe doctrine').
1910–20	Mexico: revolution and civil war.
1914–18	First World War.
1929	US stock market crash leads to world-wide economic depression, and the collapse of Latin American export earnings.
1930	Brazil: military coup overthrows elite-dominated 'Old Republic'; Getúlio Vargas becomes president.
1930–2	Military coups provoked by economic crisis in several other Latin American countries.
1941	US enters the Second World War. All Latin American countries eventually break relations with the Axis powers and ally themselves with the US.
1945	End of the Second World War.
1946	Deteriorating US–Soviet relations; onset of the cold war. Argentina: Juan Perón elected president.
1947	Mutual defence treaty (the 'Rio Pact') between US and Latin American states.
1948	Founding of the ECLA. Peru, Venezuela: military coups establish conservative dictatorships. Colombia: assassination of the populist politician Jorge Gaitán leads to destructive riots in the capital Bogotá, and *La Violencia*, several years of civil war in the countryside.
1950	Brazil: Vargas elected president on a populist platform.

1951   Argentina: Perón re-elected president.
1952   Bolivia: revolution against the 'traditional' elite of *hacienda* and tin mine owners. Argentina: death of Eva Perón.
1953   Dwight D. Eisenhower takes office as US president. End of the Korean war initiates a long-term decline in the price of Latin American raw material exports.
1954   Guatemala: US-backed rebellion overthrows the reformist government of Jacobo Arbenz. Brazil: economic and political crisis; President Vargas commits suicide. Mexico: devaluation of the peso temporarily re-establishes export competitiveness.
1955   Argentina: Perón ousted from the presidency by a military coup.
1956   Brazil: the populist Juscelino Kubitschek takes office as president, launches ambitious new ISI schemes and the construction of Brasília.
1958   Venezuela: overthrow of military dictator Pérez Jiménez. Chile: IMF-backed austerity measures provoke a political crisis. Colombia: power-sharing agreement between the two main political parties.
1959   Cuban revolution: Fidel Castro overthrows the dictator Batista, establishes a socialist regime, and breaks with the US.
1961   John F. Kennedy takes office as US president; announces the US-funded 'Alliance for Progress', to promote economic development and social reform in Latin America.
1962   Cuban missile crisis: US naval blockade against Cuba to secure the removal of Soviet nuclear missiles.
1963   Peru: election of reformist Belaúnde Terry as president. Lyndon Johnson succeeds Kennedy as US president.
1964   Brazil: 'bureaucratic-authoritarian' military coup. Chile: election of reformist Eduardo Frei as president.
1965   Dominican Republic: invasion by US forces.
1966   Argentina: 'bureaucratic-authoritarian' military coup.
1967   Bolivia: Che Guevara, associate of Fidel Castro, killed by security forces while trying to instigate Cuban-style rural guerrilla movement.
1968   Panama, Peru: radical-reformist military coups. Mexico: security forces kill several hundred student demonstrators in Mexico City.
1969   Richard Nixon takes office as US president.

1969   Argentina: riots in the city of Córdoba weaken the military government's authority. Bolivia: military coup.

1970   Chile: Salvador Allende, a Marxist, elected president. Mexico: Luis Echeverría elected president, policy becomes more populist and expansionary.

1972   Argentina: Juan Perón returns from exile. Ecuador: military coup. Nixon re-elected US president.

1973   Arab–Israeli war and OPEC action leads to four-fold oil price increase. Latin America's foreign debt US$40 billion. Chile: military coup, death of Allende, establishment of military dictatorship under General Augusto Pinochet. Argentina: Perón elected president.

1974   Argentina: death of Perón. Nixon's resignation from US presidency, succeeded by Gerald Ford.

1976   Argentina: military coup.

1977   Jimmy Carter takes office as US president.

1978   Panama: agreement of revised Canal treaty with US.

1979   Nicaragua: overthrow of dictator Anastasio Somoza by Sandinista revolutionaries.

1980   Peru: military junta relinquishes power. El Salvador: murder of reformist Archbishop Oscar Romero by a right-wing assassin.

1981   Ronald Reagan takes office as US president, backs Contras' campaign against the Sandinista government in Nicaragua.

1982   Argentina occupies the Falkland Islands (Islas Malvinas), a British colony. The islands are then retaken by a British taskforce. Mexico: the government's declaration that it cannot meet interest payments on foreign borrowing precipitates the debt crisis. Latin American foreign debt US$331 billion.

1983   Grenada: invasion by US forces to overthrow radical government. Argentina: military government relinquishes power.

1985   'Baker plan' for Latin American debt relief. Brazil: military government relinquishes power. Peru: Alan García elected president, embarks on expansionary populist economic programme. Argentina: unsuccessful '*austral* plan' for inflation control.

1986   Brazil: unsuccessful '*cruzado* plan' for inflation control.

1988   Mexico: Carlos Salinas de Gortari elected president, continues neoliberal economic policies. Venezuela: Carlos

Andrés Pérez elected president, embarks on a neoliberal programme. Chile: plebiscite vote against allowing Pinochet a further presidential term. Brazil: revised constitution devolves power from the federal government to states and municipalities, and promises increased social benefits.

1989   George Bush sen. takes office as US president. Brazil: Fernando Collor de Mello elected president, defeating the left-wing candidate Luis Inácio ('Lula') da Silva. Panama: US invasion, capture of dictator General Manuel Noriega to stand trial in US on drugs charges. Argentina: Carlos Menem, the Peronist party candidate, elected president, implements neoliberal economic policies. Chile: Patricio Aylwin elected president as candidate of the centre-left Concerctación alliance to succeed Pinochet. Venezuela: more than 300 killed in riots against IMF-prescribed austerity measures. 'Brady plan' for Latin American debt relief. Annual inflation rate 4,900 per cent in Argentina, 1,860 per cent in Brazil, 2,780 per cent in Peru, 20 per cent in Mexico, 21 per cent in Chile.

1990   Peru: Alberto Fujimori elected president, implements neoliberal economic policies. Nicaragua: Violeta Chamorro elected president, Sandinistas relinquish office.

1991   Resumption of large-scale capital inflows to Latin America, for the first time since 1982. Every country in the region except Cuba has an elected president.

1992   Brazil: President Collor de Mello impeached on corruption charges. Peru: President Fujimori dissolves Congress and suspends constitution; arrest of Abimael Guzmán, leader of the *Sendero Luminoso* guerrilla movement. El Salvador: agreement with FMLN guerrillas ends 12 years of civil war. Venezuela: Lieutenant-Colonel Hugo Chávez leads abortive military coup attempts.

1993   Bill Clinton takes office as US president. Colombia: security forces kill Pablo Escobar, a leading member of the Medellín drugs 'cartel'. Venezuela: President Carlos Andrés Pérez impeached on corruption charges. Annual net private capital inflows to Latin America reach US$60 billion.

1994   Mexico: 'Zapatista' uprising in the southern state of Chiapas; political and economic uncertainties check capital inflows, leading to the 'tequila' financial crisis; Ernesto Zedillo elected president; peso devalued. Brazil: '*real* plan' of finance minister Fernando Henrique Cardoso reduces inflation; Cardoso elected president, defeating Lula da Silva. Venezuela: Rafael Caldera elected president on a populist, anti-neoliberal platform, but soon adopts free market policies in response to a banking crisis and IMF pressure.

1995   Mexico: new austerity measures and severe economic recession; US$50 billion international support scheme for the peso. Argentina: Menem re-elected president, economic recession. Peru: Fujimori re-elected president. Latin American output per head falls by 0.3 per cent, after growing 3.3 per cent in 1994.

1996   Mexico: economic recovery, stockmarket reaches record high. Argentina: economic recovery, dismissal of finance minister Domingo Cavallo, architect of stabilization measures. Brazil: accelerated privatization programme, government rescue of insolvent banks. Guatemala: peace accords end 36 years of civil war. Annual inflation rates: Argentina nil, Brazil 11 per cent, Mexico 28 per cent, Chile 7 per cent. Latin American output per head growth: 2.0 per cent.

1997   Bill Clinton begins second term as US president. Mexico: mid-term congressional elections; the PRI governing party loses its majority in the Chamber of Deputies. Argentina: mid-term elections; the ruling Peronist party loses its majority in Congress, because of voter concerns over corruption and unemployment. Ecuador: strikes and demonstrations; Congress ousts President Abdalá Bucaram on grounds of 'mental incapacity'. Colombia: intensification of guerrilla and paramilitary violence.

1998   Colombia: Andrés Pastrana elected president; pursues a policy of negotiation with the FARC guerilla movement. Venezuela: the populist ex-army officer Hugo Chávez elected president. Brazil: economic crisis; Cardoso re-elected president, again defeating Lula da Silva; IMF agrees a $42 billion rescue package. Net private capital inflows to Latin America peak at $125 billion.

1999   Sharp economic slowdown in several Latin American countries as an after-effect of the 1997–8 East Asian and Russian financial crises. Brazil: currency devaluation and austerity measures. Argentina: election of the Radical Party – Frepaso Alliance candidate Fernando de la Rúa as president, defeating the Peronist Eduardo Duhalde. Venezuela: a new 'Bolivarian' constitution increases presidential powers.

El Salvador: elections; right-wing ARENA party retains presidency; neoliberal measures continued.

2000   Ecuador: military coup ousts president. Venezuela: Hugo Chávez re-elected president for a six year term under the new constitution. Peru: overthrow of President Fujimori following his fraudulent re-election. Mexico: the PAN candidate Vincente Fox elected president, ending seventy one years of PRI dominance. The internet stockmarket boom ends, beginning a period of economic slowdown in the developed countries. Latin America's net private capital inflows fall to \$85 billion.

2001   George W. Bush takes office as US president. Brazil: corruption scandals implicate prominent members of ruling coalition. Ecuador and Bolivia: popular protests block neoliberal measures. Nicaragua: elections; right-wing Liberal Alliance retains power, continuing neoliberal measures. Argentina: economic and political crisis; President de la Rúa resigns and is succeeded by Eduardo Duhalde; public debt default.

2002   Argentina: continuing economic crisis; output per head falls by about 10 per cent. Colombia: Alvaro Uribe elected president, on a platform of intensified military action against guerrillas and narcotics production. Peru: rioting blocks electricity privatizations. Venezuela: abortive military coup against Chávez presidency; oil workers' strike; output per head falls by about 10 per cent. Brazil: Lula da Silva wins presidential election, having moderated his anti-neoliberal stance. Latin American output per head falls by about 2 per cent.

2003   Brazil: da Silva inaugurated as president, tightens fiscal austerity and makes congressional alliances with right-wing parties. Venezuela: defeat of oil strike; President Chávez strengthens radical anti-business measures; a 16 per cent output per head decline forecast. Cuba: intensified repression of political dissidents. Argentina: the Peronist Néstor Kirchner becomes president, with 22 per cent of the first-round election vote, after Carlos Menem withdraws from the run-off ballot. Forecast net private capital inflow to Latin America: \$34 billion. Latin America's forecast output per head growth: for 2003, 0.1 per cent; for 2004, 2.4 per cent.

Glossary

abertura 'Opening': the partial relaxation of authoritarian rule and return to electoral politics allowed by the military regime in Brazil from the mid-1970s.

AFPs *Administradoras de Fondos de Previsión* (or *Pensiones*). The privately managed contributory pension funds established in Chile from 1979.

ASEAN Association of South-east Asian Nations.

balance of payments A country's international payments have three main categories, which together must be in balance: the current account, the capital account, and the movement of reserves (official gold and foreign currency holdings). The current account includes payments for goods and services, workers' remittances, interest, dividends, and grant aid. The capital account includes loans and investment. Thus, a deficit on the current account through, for example, an excess of imports over exports might be covered by a surplus on the capital account through, for example, foreign borrowing or DFI inflows. Such an outcome is often colloquially, though incorrectly, referred to as a balance of payments deficit, a usage sometimes followed in this book.

bond A fixed-interest security or loan instrument.

bureaucratic-authoritarian Term applied to Latin American military regimes established during the 1960s, especially in Brazil and Argentina, dedicated to securing social 'order' and economic development.

caudillo A national military dictator or regional leader, especially characteristic of ex-Spanish American territories in the nineteenth century.

crawling peg An exchange rate subject to frequent small officially determined changes, usually devaluations for securing export competitiveness.

creole American-born person of European descent.

current account See **balance of payments**.

devaluation See **overvaluation**.

DFI Direct foreign investment, with full enterprise control. Distinct from portfolio investment (q.v.).

ECLA(C) Economic Commission for Latin America (and the Caribbean). A United Nations agency, based in Santiago, Chile.

FTAA Free-Trade Area of the Americas. Scheme for a customs union covering all the Western Hemisphere (except Cuba), advocated by the US since the early 1990s, but not yet agreed.

garimpeiro (Brazil). Small scale 'informal sector' gold prospector and miner.

GDP Gross domestic product. A measure of national output.

GNP Gross national product. An alternative measure of national output.

hacienda A large landed estate.

ICO International Coffee Organization. A price support scheme, set up in the early 1960s, which collapsed in 1989.

IMF International Monetary Fund. An international agency based in Washington, DC. Provides short- and medium-term loans to countries with balance of payments difficulties, usually on condition that macroeconomic policy is changed.

informal sector Small-scale industrial or service activity, usually conducted by self-employed individuals (for example, street vendors), with very little capital, outside formal government regulations concerning tax payments, social security contributions, minimum wages, and safety standards.

ISI Import substituting industrialization.

LDC Less developed country.

Liberation Theology Reformist doctrine, stressing the need to achieve social justice, that became influential in the Roman Catholic Church during the 1960s and 1970s.

macroeconomic Relating to national economic aggregates, such as the balance of payments, inflation, government spending, and revenue.

maquiladoras Export-oriented assembly plants established in Mexico with access to duty-free imported inputs. Originally confined to a free trade zone along the US border, the *maquiladora* programme began in the 1960s and ended in 2001.

Mercosur 'Market of the South'. Regional trade agreement concluded in 1991 between Brazil, Argentina, Paraguay, and Uruguay.

mestizo   Person of mixed European and Indian descent.

microeconomic   Detailed aspects of economic behaviour, structure, and policy, for example educational provision, or government regulation of business.

MNC   Multinational corporation. A large capitalist enterprise, operating in several countries.

mulato   Person of mixed African and European descent.

NAFTA   North American Free Trade Agreement, concluded in 1993 between the US, Canada, and Mexico.

neo-structuralism   An approach to economic policy developed in Latin America since the late 1980s, combining the qualified acceptance of neoliberalism with a concern for improved social welfare and for raising the efficiency of state institutions.

new economic model   The more outward looking, 'free market' economic strategy advocated by neoliberals.

NGO   Non-governmental organization.

NIC   Newly industrialized country.

NSM   New social movement. Popular movement, of the type that became common under military rule during the 1970s; in general, locally based, and concerned with social welfare or human rights issues.

oligopoly   A small number of firms in a particular sector, able to collude and restrict competition.

OPEC   Organization of Petroleum Exporting Countries.

overvaluation   A national currency is said to be overvalued when its rate of exchange with other currencies makes the country's exports high priced and uncompetitive abroad, and imported goods relatively cheap. Consequently, balance of payments deficits become unsustainably large. In Latin America since 1945 overvaluation has most commonly occurred as a result of domestic price inflation continuing at a relatively high rate by international standards. For example, during the period from 1970 to 1976 the official exchange rate between the Mexican peso and the US dollar remained unchanged at 12.5 pesos = $1, while annual inflation averaged about 15 per cent in Mexico but only 7 per cent in the US. This stability of the *nominal* exchange rate, despite the difference in inflation levels, entailed a rise or appreciation of Mexico's *real effective exchange rate* (REER) relative to the US, the country's principal trading partner. Mexican exports and foreign exchange earnings were limited by the increasing overvaluation of the peso. Overvaluation can be corrected by lowering the exchange rate through a devaluation.

For example, in 1976–7 the Mexican peso was devalued from 12.5 to about 22.7 pesos = US$1. Devaluing may make a country's exports cheaper and more attractive to foreign buyers. However, the adjustment also raises the price of imports, and is thus likely to aggravate inflation. This effect can be limited by counter-inflationary austerity measures: tax increases, cuts in public spending, and the repression of workers' demands for higher pay. However, Latin American governments have often been unable to bring inflation under control, resulting in further REER increases and currency overvaluation. For example, after 1977 Mexican inflation continued at relatively high rates, and the peso had once again become considerably overvalued by the early 1980s, on the eve of the debt crisis.

Peronism   The political movement established by the Argentine populist leader Juan Perón.

populist   The term applied in Latin America to politicians who seek the support of a broad social coalition, including all classes except the landed elite, with a programme of ISI, welfare, and nationalist measures.

portfolio investment   Investment in shares or bonds, often on a short-term speculative basis, when control over an enterprise is not secured. Distinct from DFI (q.v.).

post-modernist   The term applied in this book to critics of neoliberalism who stress the value of small-scale, locally based popular collective action as a social and political strategy.

PPP   Purchasing power parity (q.v.).

PRI   *Partido Revolucionario Institucional*. The name adopted in 1946 by the party that dominated Mexican politics and government from the 1920s to the late 1990s.

purchasing power parity   (PPP). A statistical adjustment, taking account of differences between countries in living costs, sometimes made when calculating national output per head as a basis for international comparisons.

REER   Real effective exchange rate. See **overvaluation**.

sierra   Mountain, highland region.

SOE   State-owned enterprise.

Southern Cone   Argentina, Uruguay, and Chile.

statist   The term applied in this book to critics of neoliberalism who believe that the state can usefully play an active, interventionist role to promote economic development.

tequila crisis   The financial crisis that struck Mexico in 1994–5, also having a severe impact on Argentina.

terms of trade   The average price of a country's exports relative to
the average price of its imports. An increase of export prices relative to import prices represents an improvement in the terms of
trade.

TNC   Transnational corporation. See **MNC**.

Washington consensus   The consensus established by the 1980s
between the US government, the IMF, and the World Bank,
favouring neoliberal economic policies.

World Bank   An international agency, based in Washington, DC,
providing medium- and long-term loans to developing countries.

Bibliography

Abel, C. and Lewis, C. (eds) (1993) *Welfare, Poverty and Development in Latin America*, London: Macmillan. Conference papers.

—— (2002) *Exclusion and Engagement: Social Policy in Latin America*, London: Institute of Latin American Studies.

Amann, E. and Baer, W. (2002) 'Neoliberalism and its Consequences in Brazil', *Journal of Latin American Studies*, 34, Part 4: 945–59.

Andersen, L., Granger, C., Reis, E., Weinhold, D. and Wunder, S. (2002) *The Dynamics of Deforestation and Economic Growth in the Brazilian Amazon*, Cambridge: Cambridge University Press.

Baer, W. (2001) *The Brazilian Economy: Growth and Development*, 5th edition, Westport, Conn.: Praeger.

Balassa, B., Bueno, G., Kuczynski, P. and Simonsen, M. (1986) *Toward Renewed Economic Growth in Latin America*, Washington, D.C.: Institute for International Economics. Uncompromising neoliberalism.

Banuri, T. (ed.) (1991) *Economic Liberalization: No Panacea; The Experiences of Latin America and Asia*, Oxford: Oxford University Press.

Bates, R. (1997) *Open-Economy Politics: The Political Economy of the World Coffee Trade*, Princeton, N.J.: Princeton University Press.

Bennett, D. and Sharpe, K. (1985) *Transnational Corporations Versus the State: The Political Economy of the Mexican Auto Industry*, Princeton, N.J.: Princeton University Press. An exposition and critique of dependency theory, as it relates to the MNCs.

Bethell, L. (ed.) (1991) *The Cambridge History of Latin America*, vol. viii: *Latin America since 1930, Spanish South America*, Cambridge: Cambridge University Press.

—— (1994a) *The Cambridge History of Latin America*, vol. vi: *Latin America since 1930: Economy, Society and Politics*, Part 1: *Economy and Society*, Cambridge: Cambridge University Press.

—— (1994b) *The Cambridge History of Latin America*, vol. vi: *Latin America since 1930: Economy, Society and Politics*, Part 2: *Politics and Society*, Cambridge: Cambridge University Press.

—— and Roxborough, I. (eds) (1992) *Latin America Between the Second World War and the Cold War: Crisis and Containment, 1944–48*,

Cambridge: Cambridge University Press. Argues that deteriorating US–Soviet relations encouraged a swing back to authoritarian government in Latin America.

Blair, J. and Gereffi, G. (2001) 'Local Clusters in Global Chains: The Causes and Consequences of Export Dynamism in Torreon's Blue Jeans Industry', *World Development*, 29(11): 1855–1903. Optimistic views on export manufacturing in Mexico since liberalization. Contrast with Sklair (1989).

Branford, S. and Glock, O. (1985) *The Last Frontier: Fighting Over Land in the Amazon*, London: Zed Books.

Bulmer-Thomas, V. (1994) *The Economic History of Latin America Since Independence*, Cambridge: Cambridge University Press.

Buxton, J. and Phillips, N. (eds) (1999a) *Developments in Latin American Political Economy: States, Markets and Actors*, Manchester: Manchester University Press.

—— (1999b) *Case Studies in Latin American Political Economy*, Manchester: Manchester University Press.

Carothers, T. (1991) *In the Name of Democracy: U.S. Policy Toward Latin America in the Reagan Years*, Berkeley, Calif.: University of California Press. Written with insider knowledge by a former State Department official.

Chant, S. (1991) *Women and Survival in Mexican Cities*, Manchester: Manchester University Press. Female employment trends during the 1980s.

—— (2002) 'Researching Gender, Families and Households in Latin America: From the 20th into the 21st Century', *Bulletin of Latin American Research*, 21(4): 545–75.

Collins, J. and Lear, J. (1995) *Chile's Free-Market Miracle: A Second Look*, Oakland, California: The Institute for Food and Development Policy. A critique of Latin America's most celebrated neoliberal experiment. Contrast with Hojman (1993).

Crandall, R. (2002) *Driven by Drugs: U.S. Policy Toward Colombia*, Boulder, Colo.: Lynne Rienner.

Cubitt, T. (1995) *Latin American Society*, 2nd edition, London: Longman. Hostile to neoliberalism.

Díaz-Briquets, S. (1983) *The Health Revolution in Cuba*, Austin, Tex.: University of Texas Press. Puts the post-1959 Cuban mortality decline in longer term perspective.

ECLAC (1992) *Education and Knowledge: Basic Pillars of Changing Production Patterns with Social Equity*, Santiago, Chile: Economic Commission for Latin America and the Caribbean. Education in Latin America, with wider comparisons.

—— (2000) *Economic Survey of Latin America and the Caribbean 1999–2000*, Santiago, Chile: Economic Commission for Latin America and the Caribbean.

—— (2002) *Economic Survey of Latin America and the Caribbean 2001–2*, Santiago, Chile: Economic Commission for Latin America and the Caribbean.

Economist, The (2000) 4 March, 25–7: 'The Andean coca wars'.

—— (2001) 28 July, Survey: 'High Time: A Survey of Illegal Drugs'.

—— (2002) 9 March, 64: 'Air pollution in Latin America'.

—— (2003a) 22 March, 8.

—— (2003b) 22 March, 88: 'Water privatisation'.

—— (2003c) 1 November, 57–8: 'The stubborn survival of frustrated demo-crats'.

Edwards, S. (1995) *Crisis and Reform in Latin America: From Despair to Hope*, New York: Oxford University Press. A study published under the auspices of the World Bank and written by the institution's then chief economist for Latin America. Supportive of neoliberalism. Contrast with Green (1995).

Evans, P. (1979) *Dependent Development: The Alliance of Multinational, State and Local Capital in Brazil*, Princeton, N.J.: Princeton University Press. An adaptation of dependency theory.

FAO (1995) *FAO Yearbook: Production, 1994*, Rome: Food and Agriculture Organization.

Ffrench-Davis, R. (2000) *Reforming the Reforms in Latin America: Macro-economics, Trade, Finance*, Basingstoke: Macmillan. Neo-structuralist views.

Frieden, J. (1991) *Debt, Development, and Democracy: Modern Political Economy and Latin America, 1965–1985*, Princeton, N.J.: Princeton University Press. The influence of domestic interest groups on economic policy.

Gereffi, G. and Wyman, D. (eds) (1990) *Manufacturing Miracles: Paths of Industrialization in Latin America and East Asia*, Princeton, N.J.: Princeton University Press.

Gilbert, A. (1994) *The Latin American City*, London: Latin American Bureau.

Gleijeses, P. (1991) *Shattered Hope: The Guatemalan Revolution and the United States, 1944–1954*, Princeton, N.J.: Princeton University Press. A remarkable monograph, vivid and detailed.

Goertzel, T. (1999) *Fernando Henrique Cardoso: Reinventing Democracy in Brazil*, Boulder, Colo.: Lynne Rienner. The biography of a convert from Marxism to neoliberal reform, president of Brazil between 1995 and 2002.

Goodman, D. and Hall, A. (eds) (1990) *The Future of Amazonia: Destruction or Sustainable Development?*, London: Macmillan. Includes historical material.

—— and Redclift, M. (eds) (1991) *Environment and Development in Latin America*, Manchester: Manchester University Press. Argues that conventional economic strategies have proved bankrupt and unsustainable.

Green, D. (1991) *Faces of Latin America*, London: Latin America Bureau. An illustrated overview, 'left' in its assumptions.

—— (1995) *Silent Revolution: The Rise of Market Economics in Latin America*, London: Cassell. Highly critical of neoliberalism and its effects. Contrast with Edwards (1995).

Haggard, S. (1990) *Pathways from the Periphery*, Ithaca: Cornell University Press. Political economy of the East Asian 'Gang of Four', Mexico, and Brazil.

Hall, A. (1997) *Sustaining Amazonia: Grassroots Action for Productive Conservation*, Manchester: Manchester University Press.

Halperin Donghi, T. (1993) *The Contemporary History of Latin America*, London: Macmillan. Mainly politics, with some economics.

Hewitt, T., Johnson, H. and Wield, D. (eds) (1992) *Industrialization and Development*, Oxford: Oxford University Press. Statist; compares Brazil and South Korea.

Hojman, D. (1993) *Chile: The Political Economy of Development and Democracy in the 1990s*, Pittsburgh, Pa.: University of Pittsburgh Press. Sympathetic to the neoliberal reforms. Compare with Collins and Lear (1995).

Huddle, D. (1997) 'Post-1982 Effects of Neoliberalism on Latin American Development and Poverty: Two Conflicting Views', *Economic Development and Cultural Change*, 45(4): 881–97. A review and comparison of Edwards (1995) and Green (1995).

IMF (1996–2003) *World Economic Outlook*, Washington, D.C.: International Monetary Fund. Reviews current trends from a neoliberal perspective, with statistical data.

Janvry, A. de (1981) *The Agrarian Question and Reformism in Latin America*, Baltimore, Md.: The Johns Hopkins University Press. Why agrarian reform has failed to benefit the rural poor.

Jaquette, J. (ed.) (1989) *The Women's Movement in Latin America: Feminism and the Transition to Democracy*, Boston, Mass. and London: Unwin Hyman. Essays covering Brazil, Argentina, Uruguay, Peru, and Chile.

Keen, B. and Haynes, K. (2000) *A History of Latin America*, 6th edition, Boston, Mass. and Toronto: Houghton Mifflin. A survey text, hostile to neoliberalism and informed by dependency theory.

LeoGrande, W. (1997) 'Enemies Evermore: US Policy Towards Cuba After Helms-Burton', *Journal of Latin American Studies*, 29, Part 1: 211–21.

Lin, C. (1989) *Latin America vs East Asia: A Comparative Development Perspective*, Armonk, N.Y.: M.E. Sharpe. Discriminating neoliberalism; concentrates on macroeconomic policy.

Lowenthal, A. (ed.) (1991) *Exporting Democracy: The United States and Latin America, Case Studies*, Baltimore, Md: The Johns Hopkins University Press.

Maddison, A. (2001) *The World Economy: A Millennial Perspective*, Paris: Organization for Economic Co-operation and Development. Analysis and statistics of economic growth.

—— and associates (1992) *The Political Economy of Poverty, Equity, and Growth: Brazil and Mexico*, New York: Oxford University Press. Developments since 1945; a World Bank-sponsored study.

Manzetti, L. (1999) *Privatization South American Style*, Oxford: Oxford University Press. A comparative study of Argentina, Brazil, and Peru. More on causes and implementation than on consequences.

Martz, J. (ed.) (1988) *United States Policy in Latin America: A Quarter Century of Crisis and Challenge, 1961–1986*, Lincoln, Nebr.: University of Nebraska Press.

Mesa-Lago, C. (2002) 'Myth and Reality of Pension Reform: The Latin American Evidence', *World Development*, 30(8): 1309–21.

Morales, E. (1989) *Cocaine: White Gold Rush in Peru*, Tucson, Ariz.: University of Arizona Press. Social background to the drugs trade.

Moran, T. (1974) *Multinational Corporations and the Politics of Dependence: Copper in Chile*, Princeton, N.J.: Princeton University Press. The waning power of the US copper companies.

Morawetz, D. (1981) *Why the Emperor's New Clothes Are Not Made in Colombia: A Case Study in Latin American and East Asian Manufactured Exports*, New York: Oxford University Press. Neoliberal; an account sponsored by the World Bank of failure to develop export manufacturing under ISI.

Morley, M. and McGillion, C. (2002) *Unfinished Business: America and Cuba After the Cold War*, Cambridge: Cambridge University Press. Highly critical of US policy.

Murray, D. (1994) *Cultivating Crisis: The Human Cost of Pesticides in Latin America*, Austin, Tex.: University of Texas Press.

National Research Council (1993) *Sustainable Agriculture and the Environment in the Humid Tropics*, Washington, D.C.: National Academy Press. Overview, with chapters on Brazil and Mexico.

Orlove, B. (ed.) (1997) *The Allure of the Foreign: Imported Goods in Postcolonial Latin America*, Ann Arbor, Mich.: University of Michigan Press.

Page, J. (1983) *Perón: A Biography*, New York: Random House.

Panizza, F. (2000) 'Beyond "Delegative Democracy": "Old Politics" and "New Economics" in Latin America', *Journal of Latin American Studies*, 32, Part 4: 737–63.

Pietrobelli, C. (1998) *Industry, Competitiveness and Technological Capabilities in Chile: A New Tiger from Latin America?*, Basingstoke: Macmillan. Neo-structuralist views.

Psacharapoulos, G. (ed.) (1991) *Essays on Poverty, Equity and Growth*, Oxford: Pergamon Press.

Radcliffe, S. and Westwood, S. (eds) (1993) *'Viva': Women and Popular Protest in Latin America*, London: Routledge. Case studies of NSMs in which women have taken a leading role.

Reinhardt, N. and Peres, W. (2000) 'Latin America's New Economic Model: Micro Responses and Economic Restructuring', *World Development*, 28(9): 1543–66.

Roberts, B. (1995) *The Making of Citizens: Cities of Peasants Revisited*, London: Arnold. Urban social mobility and stratification in Latin America.

Rouquié, A. (1987) *The Military and the State in Latin America*, Berkeley, Calif.: University of California Press. Sophisticated analysis.

Schmitz, H. (1999) 'Global Competition and Local Cooperation: Success and Failure in the Sinos Valley, Brazil', *World Development*, 27(9): 1627–50.

Shapiro, H. (1994) *Engines of Growth: The State and Transnational Auto Companies in Brazil*, Cambridge: Cambridge University Press.

Sheahan, J. (1987) *Patterns of Development in Latin America: Poverty, Repression, and Economic Strategy*, Princeton, N.J.: Princeton University

168   *Bibliography*

Press. Takes a reformist, 'middle of the road' course between dependency theory and neoliberalism.

Skidmore, T. and Smith, P. (2001) *Modern Latin America*, 5th edition, New York: Oxford University Press. National histories, with five other chapters drawing out general themes.

Sklair, L. (1989) *Assembling for Development: The Maquila Industry in Mexico and the U.S.A.*, Boston, Mass.: Unwin Hyman. Pessimistic views on Mexican export manufacturing. Contrast with Blair and Gereffi (2001).

Smith, G. (1994) *The Last Years of the Monroe Doctrine,1945–1993*, New York: Hill and Wang. A narrative, emphasizing the doctrine's strong influence on US attitudes to Latin America until the end of the cold war.

Smith, P. (1996) *Talons of the Eagle: Dynamics of U.S.–Latin American Relations*, New York: Oxford University Press.

Stallings, B. (1987) *Banker to the Third World: U.S. Portfolio Investment in Latin America, 1900–1986*, Berkeley, Calif.: University of California Press. Puts the 1980s debt crisis in longer term perspective.

—— and Peres, W. (2000) *Growth, Employment, and Equity: The Impact of the Economic Reforms in Latin America and the Caribbean*, Washington, D.C.: Brookings Institution Press. Neo-structuralist. Summarizes a major collaborative research project sponsored by ECLAC.

Stokes, S. (2001) *Mandates and Democracy: Neoliberalism by Surprise in Latin America*, Cambridge: Cambridge University Press. Politicians who reversed populist election promises and implemented free market reforms.

Szulc, T. (1987) *Fidel: A Critical Portrait*, London: Hutchinson.

Thorp, R. (1998) *Progress, Poverty and Exclusion: An Economic History of Latin America in the 20th Century*, Washington, D.C.: Inter-American Development Bank.

Tulchin, J. and Garland, A. (eds) (2000) *Social Development in Latin America: The Politics of Reform*, Boulder, Colo.: Lynne Rienner.

Tullis, LaMond (1995) *Unintended Consequences: Illegal Drugs and Drug Policies in Nine Countries*, Boulder, Colo.: Lynne Rienner. Covers Colombia, Peru, Bolivia, Mexico, and some Asian countries. Pessimistic views on the effectiveness of supply control policies.

Vanden, H. and Prevost, G. (2002) *Politics of Latin America: The Power Game*, New York: Oxford University Press.

Ward, P. (1990) *Mexico City: The Production and Reproduction of an Urban Environment*, London: Belhaven Press. Problems of Latin America's biggest conurbation.

Wiarda, H. and Kline, H. (eds) (2000) *Latin American Politics and Development*, 5th edition, Boulder, Colo.: Westview.

Williamson, E. (1992) *The Penguin History of Latin America*, Harmondsworth: Penguin Books. A lucid overview.

Williamson, J. (ed.) (1990) *Latin American Adjustment: How Much Has Happened?*, Washington, D.C.: Institute for International Economics. Discussion of the Washington consensus and its influence. The editor coined the term 'Washington consensus'.

World Bank (1984–2003) *World Development Report*, New York: Oxford University Press. An annual review, neoliberal in its attitudes, with statistical appendices.

—— (1984b) *World Tables*, 3rd edition, Baltimore, Md: The Johns Hopkins University Press. A statistical compilation.

—— (1989b) *World Debt Tables 1989–90*, Washington, D.C.: The World Bank.

—— (2001b) *World Development Indicators*, 5th edition, Washington, D.C.: The World Bank. Statistics. Reference is made where possible to the printed edition, otherwise to the fuller CD-ROM version.

—— (2002b) *Global Development Finance 2002*, Washington, D.C.: The World Bank.

Wynia, G. (1990) *The Politics of Latin American Development*, 3rd edition, Cambridge: Cambridge University Press.

Relevant academic journals include: *Bulletin of Latin American Research,* Oxford: Elsevier Science; *Hispanic American Historical Review*, Durham, N.C.: Duke University Press; *Journal of Latin American Studies*, Cambridge: Cambridge University Press; *Latin American Research Review*, Albuquerque, N.M.: University of New Mexico Press. *The Handbook of Latin American Studies*, Austin, Tex.: Texas University Press, provides an annual bibliographical update. Current developments may be followed through the annual ECLAC, *Economic Survey of Latin America and the Caribbean*, Santiago: United Nations, neo-structuralist; *The Economist*, London: The Economist Newspaper Ltd, strongly neoliberal; *Latin America Weekly Report*, London: Latin American Newsletters; and *Keesing's Record of World Events*, Cambridge: Keesing's Worldwide. S. Collier and T. Skidmore (eds), *The Cambridge Encyclopaedia of Latin America and the Caribbean*, 2nd edition, Cambridge: Cambridge University Press, 1992, is a useful reference work.

Websites

The University of Texas Latin American Center homepage, http://lanic. utexas./edu, is the best guide on websites relating to the region. Buxton and Phillips (1999a): 205–10, (1999b): 185–90, and Vanden and Prevost (2002): *passim*, also give useful details of internet sources. The ECLAC website, www.eclac.org, has recent economic analysis and data. *Keesing's Record of World Events* since 1960 is available to subscribers at www.keesings.com.

Index